RUGBY FOOTBALL

During the
Nineteenth Century

I

Contributors

PAUL R. SPIRING is both a Chartered Biologist and Physicist. He is currently employed by the Department for Children, Schools and Families (UK) to work as Head of Biology at the European School of Karlsruhe in Germany. Paul is the joint author of two previous books entitled *On the Trail of Arthur Conan Doyle* and *A Footnote to The Hound of the Baskervilles*. In addition, he has compiled three other books entitled *Aside Arthur Conan Doyle*, *The World of Vanity Fair* and *Bobbles & Plum*. Paul is a qualified England and Wales Cricket Board Coach and he maintains a Bertram Fletcher Robinson tribute website (www.bfronline.biz).

PATRICK CASEY lives in Bristol and is employed as an I.T. Manager by a local firm of Architects. He is a past Chairman of the junior section of Clifton Rugby Football Club and maintains a website that celebrates the history of that club (www.cliftonrfchistory.co.uk). Patrick is also a qualified Rugby Football Union Coach and joint author of *For College, Club & Country - A History of Clifton Rugby Football Club*.

HUGH COOKE was born in Cardiff and educated in Stroud, so was seemingly destined to be a rugby fanatic. In a totally undistinguished and eccentric playing career, he managed not only the feat of playing in every position, but managed it in reverse order. He started off playing prop and ended up playing fly half. His ability to catch a ball and lack of speed made him ideal cannon folder. He has played the game in four countries; being introduced to new levels of pain from diverse opposing teams, such as Whitbread Brewery (a very big front row); Germany U23 (fit but clueless), until he was finally put out of his misery on a frozen pitch in Hamburg. The one ray of sunshine was to be accidentally paid someone else's boot money!

Frontispiece. 'The Webb Ellis Cup' is presented by the International Rugby Board to the winners of each Rugby Union World Cup. The inaugural tournament was held during 1987 and since that time, the competition has been restaged every four years. In January 2010, the official I.R.B. World Rankings listed ninety-five national teams.

RUGBY FOOTBALL

During the Nineteenth Century

A Collection of Contemporary

Essays about the Game

by

Bertram Fletcher Robinson

Introduced by

Patrick Casey
& Hugh Cooke

Compiled by

Paul R. Spiring

Published by
MX Publishing Ltd.,
335 Princess Park Manor,
Royal Drive,
London,
N11 3GX.

www.mxpublishing.co.uk

Cover design by
Staunchdesign,
11 Shipton Road,
Woodstock,
Oxfordshire,
OX20 1LW.

www.staunch.com

Dedication

This book is dedicated
to 'Cal' Reed and 'Sam' Reed.
I wish you future success and happiness
both on and off the rugby pitch!
In love and pride. BH.

Foreword

It is both a privilege and a pleasure to write the Foreword to this fascinating addition to the library of Rugby Books.

I am particularly delighted as Bertram Fletcher Robinson was a relation – admittedly much further up the family tree – but a relation nevertheless and one who obviously had the true ethos of the game very much in his heart. I shudder to think what he would make of today's game, with its professionalism and all the disadvantages that brings.

I admit to being firmly in Will Carling's 'Old Farts' camp. The 'amateur' game is for me, albeit one cannot stop progress.

Apart from family, I also connect with Bertram Fletcher Robinson in rugger terms. He won three Rugby Football Blues for Cambridge University during the early 1890s: today the Anti Assassins (periodically described as the poor man's Barbarians!) play Cambridge University at Grange Road every year in the Lent Term: I just happen to be the current Honorary Secretary of the AAs!

I can only describe this book as a thoroughly entertaining read – not only entertaining but instructive and it gives the reader a thorough insight into how the game was played and the spirit in which it was played at that time. Paul Spiring has done a splendid job both in researching the subject and producing such a readable volume: all credit to him.

I commend this book to all – one does not have to be a rugby enthusiast to derive enjoyment from the read, although it should be mandatory reading for all involved with the Rugby Football Union!

Graeme Marrs, M.B.E.,
Wirral,
January 2010.

Preface

In September 1979, aged eleven, I cheerfully undertook the transition from primary school to secondary school. On the first morning at 'big school', I dutifully reported to my form room to meet my new tutor, Mr. D. from South Wales. I remember being struck by the curious tone of his voice but beyond that he appeared to me to be a rather unremarkable man. Later that same day, I had occasion to meet Mr. D. again – this time on the school rugby pitch for he was also the Head of Physical Education. Our first lesson together was centred upon the art of passing and (less frequently) catching a rugby ball. It soon became apparent to me that my previously affable tutor had metamorphosed into an indefatigable bellowing machine! Demonstrably, the game of rugby can build character very speedily!

Over the next two years, I was selected by Mr. D. to play upon the wing for his (not the school's) U13 Rugby 1st XV. This proved a shrewd move on his part because I was then blessed with an impressive turn of speed – a talent that was fuelled by my determination to avoid destructive tackles. Thereafter, another P.E. Teacher discovered that I could also dash about effectively over greater distances and he encouraged me to join the District Cross Country Team. Unfortunately, there was a clash between rugby training and cross-country practice so I was compelled to focus upon my innate talent – running! However, I look back upon my brief career as a rugby player with great fondness. I believe that rugby instilled within me an appreciation for self-discipline and fair-play and that it also taught me the value of teamwork.

In September 1995, I too joined the teaching profession and since then, I have worked in a range of institutions across three different countries. Interestingly, there has been a stalwart like Mr. D. in every staffroom. Invariably Welsh, he will argue that rugby promotes both spiritual and emotional well-being in addition to developing the physique. I have even heard one former colleague argue that rugby was a factor in securing allied success during WWI and WWII – his theory being that some Tommy's had an advantage over their counterparts in so much that they had a rugby player to safeguard their back! On reflection, I feel sure that there is some merit in this view for rugby is still played extensively within the British Armed Services. Moreover, in their recent book, *For Club and Country*, Dr. Richard Hale and Patrick Casey list many heroic actions by former players of Clifton Rugby Football Club during the darkest days of the last century.

Undoubtedly, there are many other benefits to be had from playing rugby. I feel sure that each of these owes itself to the early ethos of the sport. In my efforts to learn more about the evolution of modern rugby, my attention was drawn to the book, *Rugby Football* by Bertram Fletcher Robinson. It was largely written and compiled in 1896 by leading players of the day, and whilst it focuses upon strategy and technique, its anecdotal style also conveys a sense of the spirit in which, the amateur game is still played today. Unfortunately, a good first edition of the book is rare and expensive – typically retailing for £250 ($400). Hence, I decided to republish it at a fraction of that price in the hope that this might broaden its readership and help to perpetuate the essence of rugby. I have been assisted at every stage of this venture by Graeme Marrs, Patrick Casey and Hugh Cooke and to them I say thanks.

Paul R. Spiring,
Karlsruhe, January 2010.

XII

Contents

(For further information, see page xi).

XIV

was compiled from a combination of both Masters and senior boys. During September 1888, Gardiner supported Fletcher Robinson's election to the prestigious position of '2nd Captain of School House' (a Senior Prefect).

During December 1888, Gardiner captained Devonshire XV in a match against Gloucestershire XV. The following month, he also played for Devon against a touring Maoris XV that was the precursor to the New Zealand 'All Blacks' (established 1893). This game was played at Exeter in-front of several thousand spectators and the Maoris won by a score of 2 goals and 7 tries (13 points) to nil. Fletcher Robinson witnessed this game for he later wrote on page 305 of this book that:

> One of the Devon forwards came off the field sorrowfully rubbing his leg. "What is the matter?" I asked. "Why," he said, "I came to play football, not to join in a dog fight! One of the beggars has bitten me in the calf!"

Evidently, this match left an everlasting impression upon Fletcher Robinson. However, the highlight of his school rugby career was still yet to come. On 19 December 1889, 19 year-old Fletcher Robinson was selected by Gardiner to play for a 'Newton College Past and Present XV' against the full Devonshire County XV. This match was played in front of 'a good number of spectators' at the ground of 'Newton Town' (correctly called Newton Athletic Rugby Football Club or 'The Devon All Whites' and established in 1873). The Newton College squad was photographed prior to the start of this match, which no doubt added to their sense of occasion. Despite leading the game at half-time, Newton College eventually lost this game by a score of 4 goals (12 points) to 2 tries (2 points). The full team list for both sides was as follows (*The Newtonian*, Vol. 14, Issue No. 124, pp. 180-183):

Newtonians: C.W.C. Ingles (Jesus Coll: Cambridge), (back); C.W. Hayward (Newton College), F.W. Marshall (Teignmouth), C.V. Windsor (Newton College), A.A. Bearne (Edinburgh University), (¾ backs); G.F. Davies (Newton College), E.L.L. Hammond (Newton College), (½ backs); E.N. Gardiner (Newton College), (Capt.), R.D. Williams (Emmanuel Coll: Cambridge), L.R. Biddell (Exeter), H. Osmond (Exeter), R.A. O'Neill (Newton College), B.F. Robinson (Newton College), J.C. Alsop (Newton College), W.St.A. Wake (Newton College), (forwards).

Devon County: Hayman (Exeter), (back); A.M. Sutthery (Exeter), (Capt.), M.H. Toller (Barnstaple), F.H. Davies (Plymouth Albion), (¾ backs); F.W. Herring (Tiverton), J. Davies (Torquay Athletic), (½ backs); W. Ashford (Exeter), M.W. Ball (Newton), B. Bennett (Torquay Athletic), A.G. Frith (Tiverton), C. Hawking (Torquay Athletic), Rev. T.W. Hudson (Newton), F.H. Toller (Barnstaple), S.R. Wallis (Exeter), W.S.S. Wilson (Dartmouth), (forwards).

Following this match, five Newtonians were selected to represent Devon in subsequent matches against various county teams. Moreover, Fletcher Robinson was elected to both the 'Newton College Rugby Union Committee' and 'Newton College Sports Committee'. The following assessment of Fletcher Robinson's performances for the 1st XV during the 1889/90 rugby season was published in an article entitled *Characters of the XV* (*The Newtonian*, Vol. 15, Issue No. 125, pp. 31):

ROBINSON, B.F. (1889/90). A heavy and hard-working forward. Extremely useful out of touch, though somewhat slow at times in passing.

Plate 7. The Cambridge University team that played
Oxford University (1892). Fletcher Robinson
is sat 1st right in middle row.

4) 8 November 1893 – the annual match between the
Combined Oxford & Cambridge Universities XV and the
Combined London, Southern, Western & Midland
Counties XV. It was reported by *The Times* on 9
November 1893 (p. 4). This game was played at the
Richmond Athletic Ground in Surrey and it was watched
by 'several thousand spectators'. The match referee was
E.T. Gordon. The Combined 'Varsity XV fielded seven
international players and they won this game by a score of
1 goal and 1 try (4 points) to 2 tries (2 points). The two
opposing teams were as follows:

Oxford & Cambridge Universities: **(Back);** *E* **E. Field
(Trinity, Cambridge). (¾ backs); L.E. Pilkington
(King's, Cambridge),** *W* **J. Conway-Rees (Jesus,
Oxford), W.G. Druce (Trinity, Cambridge). (½
backs); W.P. Davidson (Oxford), F. Cattell (Oxford).
(Forwards);** *E* **G.M. Carey (Exeter, Oxford), J. Baker
(Oxford),** *E* **F.O. Poole (Keble, Oxford), A.H. Colville
(Merton, Oxford),** *W* **C.B. Nicholl (Queen's,
Cambridge),** *E* **J.J. Robinson (St. John's, Cambridge),
B.F. Robinson (Jesus, Cambridge), H.D. Rendell
(Trinity, Cambridge),** *S* **W. Nielson (Clare,
Cambridge).**

XXXIX

London, Southern, Western and Midlands Counties:
(Back); J. F. Byrne (Moseley). (¾ backs); C.A. Hooper
(Middlesex Wanderers), H.P. Reynolds (Stratford-on-
Avon), J.H.C. Fegan (Blackheath). (½ backs); A.
Rotherham (St. Thomas's Hospital), T.L. Jackson (Old
Leysians). (Forwards); E. Prescott (Old Merchant
Taylors), B.H. Cattell (Moseley), G.H. Allington
(Devon County), W.W. Rice (Coventry), F. Soane
(Bath), C. Hawkings (Devon County), W.P. Wells
(Kensington), Rev. T.W.H. Carey (Leicester), W.J.
Helder (Wickham Park).

5) 13 December 1893 – the 21st annual 'Varsity Rugby
Match between Cambridge University and Oxford
University (see Plate 8). This was the first time that both
'Varsity teams used the four three-quarters formation. It
was reported in *The Times* on 14 December 1892 (p. 11).
This game was played at the Queen's Club, West
Kensington in London and it was watched by 'many
thousand' spectators. The referee was H.L. Ashmore and
the two touch judges were P. Christopherson and E.T.
Gordon. Oxford won this game by a score of 1 try (1
point) to nil. The two opposing teams fielded fifteen
international players between them and these teams were
as follows:

Cambridge University: (Back); E* E. Field (Clifton &
Trinity). (¾ backs); S* J.J. Gowans (Harrow & Clare),
S+** W. Neilson (Merchiston & Clare), W.G. Druce
(Marlborough & Trinity), L.E. Pilkington (Clifton &
King's). (½ backs); A.H. Greg (Marlborough & Trinity),
E R.O. Schwarz (St. Paul's & Christ's). (Forwards);
W*** C.B. Nicholl (Llandovery College & Queen's), E*
W.E. Tucker (Trinity College, Port Hope, Canada &
Caius), ** B.F. Robinson (Newton Abbot & Jesus), E A.F.
Todd (Mill Hill & Caius), * H.D. Rendall (Rugby &
Trinity), E F. Mitchell (St. Peter's School, York & Trinity),
S.E.A. Whiteway (Sedbergh & Trinity), H. Laing
(Wellington & Trinity).

XL

particularly interesting because it was accompanied with various endorsements as follows:

"THE ISTHMIAN LIBRARY has made more than a promising start." - Daily News.

"If succeeding issues of the new Isthmian Library Series keep up the form of the initial volume its success is certain." - Referee.

"If the following volumes of the series are equal to the present, they will, indeed, form a most useful library of sport." Birmingham Daily Post.

VOL. I. RUGBY FOOTBALL. By B.

FLETCHER ROBINSON. With Chapters by FRANK MITCHELL, R. H. CATTELL, C. J. N.FLEMING, GREGOR MACGREGOR, and H. B. TRISTRAM, and dedicated, by permission, to Mr. Rowland Hill.

Post 8vo., Cloth, 5s.

"His volume is nothing if not practical, yet it is eminently readable." - Daily News.

"Remarkably clear, practical, and modern. An excellent feature is the entrusting of each particular department of play to an acknowledged expert." - Birmingham Daily Post.

"Football now claims its handbooks, and will find one of the best in the cheerful, breezy and manly production of Mr. Fletcher Robinson." - Daily Chronicle.

"All that is worth knowing about the game will be found in this new volume." - Evening Citizen.

:

THE TIMES COLUMN OF NEW BOOKS AND NEW EDITIONS.

Vol. 1. RUGBY FOOTBALL. By B. FLETCHER ROBINSON. With Chapters by FRANK MITCHELL, R. H. CATTELL, C. J. N. FLEMING, GREGOR MACGREGOR, and H. B. TRISTRAM, and dedicated, by permission, to Mr. Rowland Hill. |Just ready.

London: A.D. Innes and co., 31 and 32, Bedford-Street, Strand.

XLV

Evidently, Fletcher Robinson's book was well received and it continued to influence both coaching and tactical play for several years after its publication. The success of *Rugby Football* can be further gauged by the fact that Fletcher Robinson was asked to replace Max Pemberton as the Editor of *The Isthmian Library* series on *Sports and Pastimes* when Pemberton resigned that position during December 1896. Between 1897 and 1901, Fletcher Robinson wrote dozens of articles for various periodicals and he also edited eight further volumes on *Sports and Pastimes* for *The Isthmian Library* (several of these volumes have recently been republished). Furthermore, Fletcher Robinson also contributed to another book about rugby, which formed part of *The Suffolk Sporting Series on Sport* (see Plate 11). This book, simply entitled *Football* was first published on 27 November 1897. On that same day, the following advertisement appeared in *The Times* (p. 12):

PUBLICATIONS TO-DAY

FOOTBALL, by
Arthur Budd, C. B. Fry, T.A. Cook, and B.F.
Robinson, Suffolk Sporting Series (Cloth 1s., paper
6d.); Lawrence and Bullen.

Football is Volume II of *The Suffolk Sporting Series on Sport* and it was edited by Henry Charles Howard (18th Earl of Suffolk and 11th Earl of Berkshire). This book is ninety-five pages in length and it is illustrated throughout with photographs. *Football* includes a section about the two codes of rugby that persisted after the N.R.F.U. split from the R.F.U. in 1895. Perhaps the most notable of the four joint authors was Arthur Budd (1853-1899). He was both a former England rugby player (1878-1881) and President of the R.F.U. (1888-1889). It is interesting to note that between 1887 and 1889, Budd also played rugby for Blackheath XV alongside Percy Illingworth (Fletcher Robinson's flatmate). The two remaining joint authors, Charles Burgess Fry and T.A. Cook, were both Oxford 'Blues' for rugby and rowing respectively.

Beyond 1901, Fletcher Robinson wrote two articles for two periodicals that make reference to Rugby Football. The first of these is entitled *The Humour of Football* and it was published in the November 1901 issue of *Pearson's Magazine* (pp. 564-568). The second is entitled *Rowing, Games, and Athletics* and it was published in the August 1906 issue of the *Windsor Magazine* (pp. 279-296). Furthermore, during 1903, Fletcher Robinson contributed a chapter on *Football at the Universities* to the second volume in a two part series of books that was entitled *Sports of the World* (see Plate 12). Fletcher Robinson's chapter deals with Rugby Football and Association Football at both the University of Cambridge and the University of Oxford. These various writings reveal that Fletcher Robinson retained a deep affection for Rugby Football long after his playing career was ended.

Plate 12. The cover of Volume II of *The Sports of the World* (edited by Frederick George Aflalo).

Additional Contributors to *Rugby Football*

Bertram Fletcher Robinson wrote eleven of the seventeen chapters for *Rugby Football*. The remaining six chapters were contributed by five other Oxbridge men: F. Mitchell (Chapter IV), R.H. Cattell (Chapter V), C.J.N. Fleming (Chapters VI & XV), G. MacGregor (Chapter VII) and H.B. Tristram (Chapter XVI). Two of these men, Mitchell and Fleming both captained the C.U.R.U.F.C. XV. All five of these men became international players; three for England and two for Scotland. When *Rugby Football* was published during October 1896, Mitchell was the current England rugby captain. Four years later, Cattell also captained England. Both Mitchell and Cattell are two of a small group of players who have captained England only once. Further biographical details about each of the five additional contributors to *Rugby Football*, is listed below.

1) Frank Mitchell (see Plate 13) was born on 3 August 1872 at Market Weighton in East Yorkshire. He was the son of Thomas, a farmer of 220 acres and Jane. Mitchell was educated at St. Peter's School in York and at Caius College, Cambridge University. He gained three Rugby Football Blues in 1893 (in a game that also featured both Fletcher Robinson and R.H. Cattell), 1894 and 1895. Mitchell also won Blues for athletics and cricket. He caused uproar whilst captaining Cambridge in the 'Varsity Cricket Match of 1896 when he ordered a bowler to give away extras so that Oxford would not have to follow-on. This action led to the law being changed so that enforcing the follow-on became voluntary.

Plate 13. The England team that played Scotland on 9 March 1895. (L-R) Back Row: H.W. Finlinson (Blackheath), J.F. Byrne (Moseley), C. Thomas (Barnstaple), F. Mitchell (Cambridge University), R.M. Carey (Oxford University), W.B. Thomson (Blackheath), T.H. Dobson (Bradford). Seated: W.E. Tucker (Cambridge University), R.H. Cattell (Moseley), W.E. Bomet (Richmond), S.M.J. Woods [Captain] (Bridgwater and Blackheath), E.W. Taylor (Cambridge University), F.O. Poole (Oxford University). Ground: J.H.C. Fegan (Blackheath), E.M. Baker (Oxford University).

Mitchell played rugby for England on six occasions. On 14 March 1896 he captained England during his last international against Scotland at Hampden Park, Glasgow. Interestingly, this match featured four of the contributors to *Rugby Football*. In addition to Mitchell there was Cattell for England and both Fleming and MacGregor for Scotland. England lost 11-0 with Fleming scoring a try for Scotland. This was England's fourth successive defeat to Scotland.

Mitchell also played international cricket for both England (1898/99) and South Africa (1912). At the time of writing, he remains one of only fourteen players to have played Test Cricket for more than one country. He also played Association Football for Sussex.

Frank Mitchell died aged 63 years on 11 October 1935 at Blackheath in London.

2) Richard Henry Burdon Cattell was born on 23 March 1871 at Erdington in Birmingham. He was the son of Thomas, a farmer of 559 acres, and Maria. Cattell was educated at Trinity College in Stratford-upon-Avon and Exeter College at Oxford University. He gained a Rugby Football Blue during 1893 in a game that also featured both Fletcher Robinson and Frank Mitchell. Cattell also played for Blackheath, Moseley, Barbarians and Midland Counties.

Cattell and Mitchell both featured in the England side that played Scotland on the 9 March 1895 (see Plate 13). This turned out to be the last game that was contested by an England side prior to the formation of the breakaway Northern Rugby Football Union. The R.F.U. foresaw this split and they responded by selecting more Oxbridge players and fewer Northern players for the game against Scotland.

Cattell won seven caps for England. During 1900, he made his only appearance as captain of England in an international match that was played at Kingsholm in Gloucester. This was also Cattell's final match for England. Cattell also played Association Football for Welwyn A.F.C. (1898-1903) and then Tring Town (till 1906).

During 1897, Cattell was ordained as an Anglican Priest. Between 1909 and 1923, he was installed as Perpetual Curate at St. Michael and All Angels, Sunnyside with St. John, Broadway. Thereafter, Cattell was appointed Rector of Watlington (1923-1928), and of Warham St. Margaret, Norwich (1928-1948). Cattell also served as a Chaplin to the Armed Forces during World War I.

Richard Cattell died aged 77 years on 19 July 1948.

3) Charles James Nicol Fleming (see Plate 14) was born on 5 April 1868. He was educated at Fettes College in Edinburgh and at Queen's College, Oxford University. Between 1887 and 1890, Fleming gained four Rugby Football Blues (two of these matches also featured G. MacGregor). Thereafter, he also played for Scotland and gained three caps (1896-1897). Later, Fleming served as the President of the Scottish Rugby Union.

Between 1893 and 1900, Fleming worked as an Assistant Master at his old school, Fettes College. Thereafter, he joined the Ministry of Public Instruction in Egypt and then the Sudan Civil Administration. Fleming was appointed Her Majesty's Inspector of Schools for Scotland during 1903.

Charles Fleming died aged 80 years on 13 November 1948 at Castle Douglas in Dumfries and Galloway.

Plate 14. Oxford University 1890. (L-R) Back Row: F.I. Cowlishaw, A.M. Paterson, W. Rice-Evans, R.W. Hunt, A.R. Kay, S.E. Wilson, W.H. Parkin. Seated: R.F.C. de Winton, E.H.G. North, C.J.N. Fleming (Captain), J.H.G. Wilson, P.R. Clauss. Ground: R.G.T. Coventry, E. Bonham-Carter, P.R. Cadell.

4) Gregor MacGregor (see Plate 15) was born on 31 August 1869 at Merchiston in Edinburgh. He was educated at Uppingham School and Jesus College, Cambridge University. MacGregor gained two Rugby Football Blues during 1889 and 1890, and he also gained four Cricket Blues. He played rugby for Scotland on three occasions and was an original member of the Barbarians. MacGregor played cricket for England on eight occasions and captained Middlesex County Cricket Club between 1898 and 1907.

It is perhaps worth noting that during the 1889 'Varsity Rugby Match, MacGregor played alongside Percy Holden Illingworth. The latter man would later rent rooms in London with Bertram Fletcher Robinson (1896-1901). Moreover that same 'Varsity Rugby Match also featured C.J.N. Fleming (Oxford University), who contributed two chapters to *Rugby Football*. The Oxford XV won this match by a score of 1 goal and a try (4 points) to nil.

Gregor MacGregor died aged 49 years on 20 August 1919 at Marylebone in London.

Plate 15. Cambridge University 1889. (L-R) Back Row: P.H. Illingworth, E.C. Langton, W. Wotherspoon, G. MacGregor, F.C. Bree-Frink, J.W. Bowhill, A.L. Jackson, C.E. Fitch. Seated: R.L. Aston, W. Martin Scott, P.H. Morrison (Captain), S.M.J. Woods, P.T. Williams. Ground: T.W.P. Storey, J. Smith. Absent: J.C. McDonnell.

5) Henry Barrington Tristram (see Plate 16) was born on 5 September 1861 at Greatham in County Durham. He was the son of one Henry Baker Tristram and was affectionately referred to as 'Tim'. H.B. Tristram's grandfather was Henry Baker Tristram, a Priest who devoted his life to the Church, ornithology and travel writing. He was affectionately referred to as 'the birdman canon'.

H.B. Tristram received his schooling at Loretto School (1870-1873 & 1879-1881) and Winchester College (1875-1879). Thereafter, he was educated at Hertford College, Oxford University. Tristram gained three Rugby Football Blues between 1882 and 1884. He also played rugby five times for England and was never once on the losing side during his international career. Tristram also played cricket for both Oxford University and Durham County Cricket Club.

Between 1886 and 1887, Tristram was a Classics Master at Newton Abbot Proprietary College in Newton Abbot (where he taught Bertram Fletcher Robinson). In 1887, he left to become an Assistant Master at Loretto School. Later, Tristram was promoted to Vice-Gerent (1891-1903) and Headmaster (1903-1908). During 1911, he had a book published that is entitled *The History of Loretto School*. Tristram also worked as a House Master at St. Paul's School in London (1909-1912). However, ill-health compelled him to retire and he subsequently relocated to Jersey in the Channel Islands.

Henry Tristram died aged 85 years on 1 October 1946 at St. Helier in Jersey.

Plate 16. H. B. Tristram (circa 1903).

RUGBY FOOTBALL

OVERTAKEN

The Isthmian Library, No. 1.

RUGBY
FOOTBALL

BY

B. FLETCHER ROBINSON

ILLUSTRATED

Edited by Max Pemberton

LONDON
A. D. INNES & CO.
BEDFORD STREET
1896

TO

MR. G. ROWLAND HILL,

RUGBY FOOTBALL IN ENGLAND,

I DEDICATE

THIS BOOK.

EDITOR'S FOREWORD.

THE Isthmian Library of Sports and Pastimes has for its chief object the instruction of the novice who is the master neither of sporting technique nor of any considerable athletic knowledge. It is our hope to win many friends from the ranks of those who are regular frequenters of the playing-fields, but are unable to find there a demonstration of those first principles upon which all athletic success is based. We shall seek to make these books true primers of sport. They will take nothing for granted, nor will they assume even elementary achievements. At the same time, we venture to believe that the authors who have given us their most able and welcome assistance are so well entitled to speak, each for his own sport, that

the attention of the expert will be called to the
series.   And even he, we hope, may find in it
something which he may read to his profit.

Nothing is more characteristic of the sport of
our time than the love of change which distinguishes its devotees.   The game of to-day is the
tradition of to-morrow.   The man who succeeds
must ever reckon with the ephemeral moods which
this or that school seeks to enforce.   In venturing
to put before the public a new series of didactic
books, we shall endeavour to say the ultimate
word so far as time and circumstance will permit
it to be said.   Our volumes will, we trust, deal
with all that is newest, and with all that is best in
the teaching of the hour.   Nor will they be forget-
ful of those great and abiding traditions which
are the precious and well-beloved inheritance of
the British sportsman.

MAX PEMBERTON.

CONTENTS.

RUGBY FOOTBALL.

CHAPTER I.

THE PAST.

WHAT was the origin of football?
Many have attempted to answer this
question, but no one can be said to
have succeeded. Some enthusiasts
have taken their historical researches
as far back as the "Odyssey," and
there found, to their delight, that
Nausicaa of the white arms was engaged in a
game of ball with her maidens when the goodly
Odysseus appeared, very much *en déshabillé*, before
her. Why they considered this worth chronicling remains shrouded in mystery. Possibly their
eager eyes may have discerned in it the origin of
passing, or of the new movement in the direction
of football for ladies! Unfortunately, there is

nothing further to show that this was not the germ of cricket, or lawn tennis, or even baseball. On the whole, it will be safer to say that Homer was not conversant with football. Advancing a few centuries, our friends next discovered that the Romans were in the habit of playing with an inflated ball called the *follis*. It is true that the game consisted in striking it into the air with the hands. But that is a mere matter of detail; for, as one of them gravely asserts, "it is hardly to be believed that it should never have occurred to a man playing with the *follis* to kick it with his foot when his arms were tired." It may also have occurred to a man to strike it with some form of a bat. Yet, in spite of this ingenious—or, rather, ingenuous—argument, it cannot be safely affirmed that either cricket or football were recognized sports in ancient Rome. A game of Rugby football as played in the sixties would have been immensely popular in the Colosseum. No record of such a pastime remains, however—not even the tombstone of the referee!

From what we know of our Saxon forefathers, it is much more probable that it is to them, and to them alone, that we owe the game of football.

War was their exercise, rough practical joking
their humour. Primitive football, with its hard
knocks and its horse-play, combined the two. It
was an ideal game for them ; and when the growth
of law and order limited their possibilities in the
direction of free fights, they found in it all that
was necessary to counteract the peaceful absurdi-
ties of civilization. There is no doubt that for
many centuries football games were somewhat
bloodthirsty affairs. A match between two vil-
lages not unfrequently ended in a riot. The
Normans could not understand the pleasure that
the lower orders found in these contests, and the
Norman kings strongly objected to football riots
—"hustlings over great balls," as Edward II.
called them. To a Norman gentleman there were
only two forms of exercise—hunting and the use
of arms. A young man required nothing more to
fill up an athletic day. Heavy armour was not to
be lightly carried, nor a lance and sword easily
wielded without constant practice. Thus it came
about that football was the game of the people,
confined to those classes that were debarred
from breaking each other's heads in tournaments
and similar pastimes. But this, again, was not

at all pleasing to warlike sovereigns, who considered that their sturdy subjects should have
been spending their time in shooting at targets,
instead of forsaking the bow to indulge in "useless,
unlawful, and importune games," as bouts at football were designated. The Scotch monarchs hated
these "hustlings" just as much as their brothers
of England, and James III. decreed that four
times in every year they should be "utterly
cryed down." However, there was no use "cry-
ing" over spilt milk. In both kingdoms the
delight in a rough and tumble was bred in the
bone. The kings could pile on ordinance after
ordinance, the bishops could preach countless
sermons, the scholars could sneer so subtly that
no one understood them save themselves; but
football had come to England, and, to use an
Americanism, football had "come to stay." There
was little skill in the game; the rules were of
the vaguest; yet, despite the fact that the
strongest man was the best player, the English
love of fair play rarely allowed the game to become merely an exhibition of brutality. Accidents
were, without doubt, of frequent occurrence, but
they were the result of chance, not, as the majority

of mediæval writers would have us believe, of malice aforethought.

Several descriptions of the rules which governed the game in different districts have been preserved; but they are hardly of very great interest to the football player of to-day. The comments with which they are accompanied are, however, distinctly amusing. Sir Thomas Elyot, a worthy baronet who flourished under the Tudors, considered that in football there was "nothing but beastlie furie and extreme violence, whereof procedeth hurte, and consequently rancour and malice do remain with them that be wounded, whereof it is to be put in perpetual silence." There is some truth in what he says. Often have I seen a listless player suddenly awake to "beastlie furie" on receiving a provocative hack, and become a terror to his adversaries, proceeding to treat them with "extreme violence." "Rancour and malice" are by no means conspicuous by their absence in the modern football cup-tie. But perhaps the Puritan Stubbes attacks the game in the most determined manner. He begins reasonably enough by calling it a "friendlie kind of fight;" and I do not quarrel with the description, for that is

B

exactly what it was.   Unfortunately, he next proceeds to give full play to his imagination, and uses
a great deal of strong language, not only refusing
to call it a recreation, but insisting that it is
nothing but a "bloody and murthering practice;"
in fact, a "develishe" business altogether.   He is
much agitated by the method in which this terrible
game is played.   It causes a man "to lye in
waight for his adversarie, seeking to overthrow him
and piche him on his nose, though it be on hard
stones"—a most painful operation undoubtedly,
and liable to produce "rancour and malice" in
"he that be wounded."   The eloquent Stubbes
apparently saw and feared this danger, for in an
agony of pious horror he complains that from these
proceedings come "brawling, murther, homicide,
and great effusion of blood, as experience daily
teaches."   Their method of tackling was, he considered, even more objectionable.   The fact that
many are injured is, he thinks, "no marveille,
for they have the sleights to meet one betwixt
two, and to dash him against the hart with their
elbowes, to butt him under the short ribs with
their gripped fists, and with their knees to catch
him on the hip and piche him on his neck, with

a hundred such murthering devices." There is a suspicious knowledge of detail about this that would almost induce us to believe that either our Puritan friend was a player himself on the sly, or else that he was an interested spectator of these same "murthering devices."

The good citizens of Manchester objected to the game for quite another reason; for the municipal body stated, in 1608, that "whereas there has been heretofore great disorder in our toune of Manchester, and the inhabitants thereof greatly wronged and charged with makinge and amendinge of their glasse windows, broken yearlye and spoiled by a companye of lewd and disordered persons using that unlawful exercise of playing with the ffote ball in ye streets of ye said toune, breakinge many men's windowes and glasse at their pleasures and other great enormyties," they would fine those persons twelve pence should they offend in like manner again. The picture of a fat elder of the town gazing indignantly through his broken panes—and glass was expensive in those days—at the lewd and disordered football players rises distinctly before me. It reminds me of a story of a celebrated undergraduate, well known for his

brilliant eccentricities, who was passing through
his college in company with a lady visitor.
"There are my tutor's rooms," he said, pointing
them out. Then, stooping, he picked up a pebble
and tossed it through a pane. " And there," he
continued, as a red and irate face appeared—
" there is my tutor."

After the criticism of Stubbes, the remark of
Sir W. Davenant that football "is not very con-
veniently civil " seems mild indeed. Besides, he
is quite right in his opinion—it is not. The cry
of disapproval has so far been unanimous, and
it is thus refreshing for the enthusiastic Rugby
player to light upon one writer who had the
common sense to see that there were many good
points about the game. Carew, a West-country
man, as his name denotes, tells us that football
was played regularly in Cornwall at the com-
mencement of the seventeenth century. " I cannot
well resolve," he concludes, after a minute description of the game, "whether I should the more
commend the game for its manhood and exercise,
or condemn it for the boisterousness and harm
that it begetteth ; for as on the one side it makes
their bodies strong, hard, and nimble, and puts a

courage into their hearts to meet an enemy in the face ; so, on the other part, it is accompanied by many dangers, some of which do even fall to the player's share ; for the proof whereof, when the hurling (*i.e.* the game) is ended you shall see them retiring home as from a pitched battle with bloody pates, bones broken and out of joint, and such bruises as serve to shorten their days, yet all in good play, and never attorney or coroner troubled for the matter." Here, then, was one Englishman at least who could appreciate the fact that a few hard knocks given and taken in fair play are not such terrible things, after all. The mention of the coroner is, I must admit, rather awe-inspiring ; but, then, it might only have been a West-country joke on the part of Carew.

Later writers than those I have mentioned still speak of the game as a pure rough-and-tumble struggle, with few rules and many accidents. Strutt, the great historian of English sports, writing in 1801, tells us that "when the exercise becomes exceedingly violent the players kick each other's shins without the least ceremony, and some of them are overthrown at the hazard of their limbs." Glover, again, has something to say

of the game as played in Derbyshire in 1829.
" Broken shins, broken heads, torn coats and lost
hats," he writes in horror, " are among the minor
accidents of this fearful contest, and it frequently
happens that persons fall, owing to the intensity of
the pressure, fainting and bleeding beneath the
feet of the surrounding mob. But it would be
difficult to give an adequate idea of this rutheless
sport. A Frenchman passing through Derby
remarked that if Englishmen called this playing,
it would be impossible to say what they would call
fighting." How surprised the excellent Glover
would have been if he had been told that before
the century was out numbers of Frenchmen would
have grown wildly enthusiastic about this " fearful
contest"! Another remark of his is distinctly
amusing. "The crowd," he relates in astonish-
ment, " is encouraged by respectable persons, who
take a surprising interest in the result of the day's
sport, urging on the players with shouts, and even
handing to those who are exhausted oranges and
other refreshment." Surprising indeed for you,
Mr. Glover, in 1829! What would you have said
could you have been set down in the Oval in 1887,
but fifty-eight years after you published your

excellent work, and there seen the Heir Apparent to the English throne, surrounded by large numbers of presumably "respectable" people, watching the progress of a football game with the liveliest interest? What would you have thought of a sportsmanlike prince consenting to become Patron of a Union that had for its object the encouragement of this "rutheless sport"? It is impossible to tell. But if such proceedings would have seemed incomprehensible to Glover, they would have dealt a blow to our friend Stubbes from which he would never have recovered, and which would inevitably have driven him into socialism or some such form of harmless, but bellicose, insanity.

From the above criticisms a general idea can be obtained of football in its early days. A game so devoid of athletic skill and science could not be expected to last. It had never taken any firm hold on the wealthier or better educated classes, and even among the rustics and apprentices, who risked life and limb so recklessly, it was rather a customary form of spending certain high days and holidays throughout the year, than a definite game to be played regularly. Manly sport though it was, it was too barbarous for an advancing civilization, and towards the middle of the present century its popularity had so far waned that it was usually spoken of as an interesting relic of the customs of elder days. It still lingered amongst the public schools. But each school had its own rules, which had been drawn up to suit the requirements of the narrow bounds of the school recreation grounds as they then existed. Outside the schools, it was confined to country districts where a football would be kicked about for an hour or two on certain holidays. The ball was generally a bladder, and the object of the game, if game it can be called, was to find an excuse for an extra consumption of beer. The old enthusiasm which produced such catastrophes amongst the players, and such violent language from the writers, had died out. No gentleman seems to have thought of playing after leaving school. At the Universities it was unheard of as a game for "men." A proposal to play football would have seemed just as absurd as a challenge to a match at marbles on the Senate House steps, a spot which Cambridge holds especially sacred from such profanations.

How Rugby football emerged from this shadow, and became one of the most popular of sports amid all classes in modern England, I will relate in the next chapter.

CHAPTER II.

THE PRESENT.

"I AM well aware," wrote Mr. Caspar Whitney in his "Sporting Pilgrimage"—an account of the wanderings of an American through Oxford, Cambridge, and the shires—"that I shall be exposing myself to a charge of triteness by proclaiming what every one already knows, that the average Britisher is an athlete, the English nation an athletic one, and its subjects, both men and women, more universally and generally imbued with the athletic spirit than those of any other race on earth." Without wishing to exhibit an undue amount of patriotic pride, I cannot but agree with our American admirer in his estimate of the England of to-day. Yet, as a matter of fact, our athleticism is about as modern as our railways.

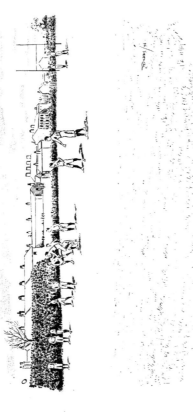

A FREE KICK

What exercise, for instance, did our young men take during the winter months some fifty years ago—not the young men who could afford to hunt and shoot, but the average young men in the towns, who could get away from their work for one or two afternoons a week ? They played billiards a little ; they skated occasionally when the ice was in good condition ; now and then, if they were of a very sporting turn of mind, they attended a cock-fight, or sat open-mouthed behind the ropes of a prize-ring. In the novels of Dickens or Thackeray we read of no other forms of athletic amusement. That most lugubrious of bores, William Cobbett, when considering the advantages of sports for young men, wrote, "A town life which many people are compelled from the nature of their calling to lead, precludes the possibility of pursuing amusements of this description. Young men in towns are, generally speaking, compelled to choose between books on the one hand, or gambling and the play-house on the other." Yet to-day Mr. Whitney, of the jealous U.S.A., is afraid of being called trite for proclaiming that our nation is athletic to the backbone.

What was it, then, that brought about the change

in our habits? It is a difficult question to answer
satisfactorily. Perhaps it was that the love of
fresh air and healthy exercise is bred in our bones;
that as the towns grew larger, and the country
more distant for the dwellers amongst bricks and
mortar, a game became the only form of exercise
possible; that better regulations and an energetic
police forbade rough bouts at various forms of
football in the streets, and an organized game
with a settled playing field became necessary. It
was a winter game that was required, for cricket
and rowing were rapidly growing in popularity
during the summer. Such was the state of affairs
when young men fresh from Rugby and Marlborough, and other great schools where football
had never died out, set an example by continuing
to play the game they had learned to love. As
the play became more scientific and less brutal,
other young men anxious to get exercise joined
the clubs that had already been formed, or started
fresh ones of their own. To be a famous athlete
became an honourable distinction instead of another
term for what a celebrated Cambridge dean used
to describe as a " nasty, fast man." As the number
of clubs increased, the competition for places in

the teams became exceedingly keen, and in a few years the players of Rugby football were to be reckoned in thousands. An organization was required to control and legislate for them. On the 26th January, 1871, a party of members of London and suburban clubs met and resolved that the formation of a Rugby Football Union was desirable. From that moment the position of the game was assured. Steadily it grew in favour, until it emerged from the shadows of old prejudices and became equal, if not superior, in popularity to any other member of the great family of English Sports.

In 1865 there were but fifteen to twenty clubs round London playing Rugby football. Nearly all the teams were composed of young men who had previously learnt the game at the two great football schools, Rugby and Marlborough. The Richmond team in that year, for instance, was entirely composed of Old Rugbeans and Old Marlburians. The rules were in a very uncertain state, and the opposing captains often met to decide the minor points before the game commenced. The grounds about London were unenclosed, and the spectators seem to have wandered

about at their own sweet will. Indeed, a smart
half often availed himself of the protection of
the crowd to dash in near the touch-line before
the unfortunate back opposed to him could find
out exactly where he was. The number of players
was uncertain, but usually twenty a side. The
off-side laws were very lax, and some clubs would
send down an advance guard of forwards to protect
the man running with the ball. This fact is rather
interesting, because the Americans adopted the
same plan, and have never changed it. In Yankee
football the protection of the man with the ball is
all important, and for this purpose their systems
of wedges and lines of covering forwards were
invented. The scrummages were long, tedious
bouts of hard shoving. The men did not put their
heads down, but stood upright and hacked and
pushed their way blindly forward.

This hacking was the worst feature of the game.
It was useful in one respect, for without it the ball
might never have emerged from the forest of legs
which concealed it. It seems to have originated
at Rugby school. The hacking there was indeed
of a terrible nature. To hack hard and take your
punishment manfully seems to have been the end

and object of the play. Two boys would often be seen steadily hacking each other long after the ball and the forwards had passed to the other side of the ground. Personal disputes were sometimes settled in this rough and ready fashion. Of course some elderly football players, whose old triumphs, as seen through the softening haze of the past, awake nothing but pleasant memories, are still willing to contend that the hacking system was neither dangerous nor brutal. This is simply absurd. Many an Old Rugbean can show scars existing to-day which are the relics of wounds received under the old barbarous rules. There is no doubt that accidents were of very common occurrence, and that the majority of them were due to hacking and hacking alone. The first upward step that Rugby football made from brutality to science was the abolition of the entire system of hacking an opponent in the scrum or tripping him up when he was running with the ball. Mr. Arthur C. Guillemard, in Mr. Marshall's "History of Football," relates an anecdote from his personal experience which throws more light on this style of play than anything I can say. "I well remember," he writes, "seeing the crack

'hack' of one season, after coming through the
scrummage, finish off his triumphal march by
place-kicking the half-back in front of me clean
off his legs"—a pleasant picture of football as it
was played in the sixties.

Of course, under such rules as these, football
acquired a most unenviable reputation. The
letter of "A Surgeon" to the *Times* roused a
mass of correspondents from all parts of the
country. Exaggerated statements were made on
both sides. Some football players declared that
they had played for years, and never seen a worse
accident than a cut knee. On the other hand, the
opponents of the game insisted upon styling it
"dangerous," which it undoubtedly was, and "un-
manly," which it undoubtedly was not. It was
even threatened that Parliament should be peti-
tioned to abolish so dangerous a pastime. *Punch*
warmly supported the malcontents, and many
may remember the picture representing a sprawl-
ing, hacking, struggling crowd of players, on which
"Mr. P." expressed a forcible opinion.

Without reform the game would have been in
a bad way; but better times were in store. In
1871, as I have already mentioned, the Rugby

Union was formed, and shortly afterwards the
evil practice of hacking was abolished, to the joy
of all true lovers of the game, and the loudly
expressed disgust of those who trusted in their
bootmakers to bring them football fame.

Yet for some time the style of play continued to
be of a ponderous nature, and, so it would seem,
distinctly unattractive to the uninitiated. Hacking
had, at least, forced the ball out of the scrummage ;
but now the game consisted of long bouts of hard,
blind shoving. Half the forwards had but a vague
idea as to where the ball was, and often a half-
back had secured it, and was running strongly
thirty yards away before the closely packed giants
in the scrummage realized the fact, and began
slowly to disentangle themselves. In 1876 a great
improvement was effected when, at the request of
Scotland, where football was rapidly increasing in
popularity, the number of players in the International matches was reduced from twenty to
fifteen. The clubs followed the example thus set
them. The game became faster and more open,
although the scrummages were still grievously pro-
longed. The rules were altered for the better. It
was ordered that a player running with the ball

C

should, when tackled, immediately put it down,
instead of either struggling on with half a dozen
opponents attached to him, or delaying matters
until his own forwards had time to come straggling
up to his assistance. To suit the faster style of
play, the position of the players behind the scrummage was changed. The two halves had been all-
important under the old rules. To them had been
entrusted the brunt of the work in running, kicking, and tackling. Now, however, attack and
defence were mainly in the hands of the three-
quarter line, which was increased from one to two
players, and subsequently to three or four. The
half became practically a conduit-pipe to transfer
the ball to the men behind him. His position was
still most important, for the strongest part of a
chain is its weakest link ; but he ceased to be the
only man to whom frequent chances of "gallery"
play were afforded.

In 1882, the Oxford team, at the suggestion of
the famous Arthur Budd, and under the direction
of the equally famous Harry Vassall, developed the
passing system amongst halves and three-quarters.
Long, low passing amongst the forwards was also
introduced. The great half-back, A. Rotherham,

who was a member of the team, showed to the
football world what the true duties of a half-
back were. He was not to neglect the three-
quarters, as in the early days of the Rugby game,
nor was he to consider himself merely a conduit-
pipe, as was the tendency of some of the half-
backs of his time. A happy medium between
the two was to be aimed at. By personal example, Rotherham proved that his system of
making openings for three-quarters, and then
passing to them, was the correct and only system
for half-backs who aspired to the highest football honours. Of late years the forwards have
perfected the art of wheeling and screwing the
scrummages, and of taking the ball down the field
by a series of rushing dribbles—of all things the
most difficult for a half or three-quarter to meet
and check. Finally, the passing game has become
thoroughly understood by the three-quarters. In
the great majority of clubs, and in all International
matches, one more has been added, making their
number four instead of three. Football players
of the modern school are nearly unanimous in
praising this innovation. When it was introduced
from Wales it was bitterly opposed, and veterans

amongst us declared that it was ruining the game. On the contrary, however, it has turned out a distinct improvement, a further step in the direction of scientific play.

Nothing has done more to keep up the public interest in football than the International matches. For such matches Great Britain is excellently situated. England and Wales, Scotland and Ireland, have never so far merged into a common whole as to lose their national characteristics and national sympathies. The result is that many people who know little or nothing about the game will take a keen interest in these International contests. It is not too much to say that when Scotland, for instance, maintains an unbeaten record, the whole nation rejoices in her victories. It was in 1871 that the first match, England *v.* Scotland, was played at Edinburgh. In 1874 a challenge was received from Ireland, which was accepted for the following season. Ireland was easily beaten for many years, but in 1887 scored her first victory, to her great delight. Her forwards have always been a powerful body of men, and her defeats have in the majority of cases been the result of deficiencies behind the scrummage.

At present she is far behind both England and
Scotland in the number of her successes in the
International matches. England she has beaten
three times to the sixteen victories scored against
her. Scotland has beaten her fifteen times, and
has only been defeated twice, two matches being
drawn. Last season, however, her team was of
the highest excellence. England and Wales fell
before her, and Scotland was lucky to be able to
retire with a draw.

Ireland has had many difficulties to contend
with. Rugby football is practically confined to
the north-east of Ireland and the "English pale,"
as it used to be called, round Dublin. Her clubs
have been cut off by the boisterous Irish Sea from
meeting the best of the English teams with any
regularity. It is difficult for a club to learn to
win until it has been constantly beaten by clubs
better than itself, from whom, though it loses
matches, it may gain experience. Moreover, the
sinews of war in the "distressful" country have,
unfortunately, often proved insufficient to meet the
demands made upon them. A form of Irish football must be mentioned that has long flourished in
the country districts. A wit has divided it into

three kinds, each playing with separate rules. Of
these, the first is the game where you kick the ball;
the second, where you kick the man if you cannot
kick the ball ; and the third, which is purely Gaelic
and most popular, where you kick the ball if you
cannot kick the man.   I am surprised that no
patriot has started a league under Gaelic rules ; referees to be appointed from Committee-room No. 15.

Between England and Scotland the struggles
have been veritably those of giants, and the tabu-
lated results for the last twenty years show how
close the fight has been.   Eight matches a-piece
is the score of the two countries, while no less
than seven games have been drawn.   The Scottish
forwards have always been the mainstay of the
Scottish team.   Drawn from the schools where
the importance of sound, hard-working scrummagers is realized more than in our own country,
they have time after time shattered the English
front rank, and left to the English backs the
difficult task of stemming the torrent of defeat.   As
a general rule, the English backs and the Scotch
forwards would form an ideal team.   With the
spread of Rugby football abroad, we may some
day see such a combination figure in the field.

It was not until 1880 that Wales first challenged
England. For some time football had been
making steady progress amongst the thickly
populated mining and shipping districts in the
south ; but at the time of the challenge—and as a
matter of fact at the present moment—the football
of Wales is represented by four great clubs—
Swansea, Llanelly, Cardiff, and Newport. It is
naturally surprising to find that Wales, with her
handful of players, has made such a brave fight
against her powerful rivals. The reasons are, I
consider, three in number. In the first place,
though her clubs are but few they are all of the
highest football merit. The competition between
them arouses the greatest enthusiasm. Their
position has always enabled them to play the
crack metropolitan clubs, and, unlike the Irishmen, notice and assimilate any improvement that
the Englishmen have originated. In the second
place, the same style of play is to be found in all
the Welsh clubs ; and when it comes to selecting
an International team, the players chosen already
know each other's style, and work together with
that machine-like accuracy that distinguishes their
club matches. Lastly, the " Taffies " have always

shown a distinct genius for football.	Many a time
have their rivals been absolutely nonplussed by
their tactics.	It was the Welshmen that invented
the four three-quarter system, and, with all due
deference to our famous English clubs, it is the
Welshmen alone who play the four three-quarter
game as it should be played.	Let us turn for a
moment to their opponents.	We find International
teams of individually good players who yet cannot
combine.	The Welsh team is never a scratch
fifteen of good men, each doing his best for himself, as is so often the case with the team that
England puts into the field.	Every experienced
football player knows the advantage of combina-
tion over individual merit.	At the same time,
England is far ahead of the little Principality,
having won ten matches to two credited to Wales,
while one has been drawn.	Scotland, the great
rival of English football supremacy, has also run
up a long list of successes over Wales.	She has
now won nine matches, and lost four, while one
has been drawn.	Between Ireland and Wales,
the junior members of the football family, the
struggle has been close and exciting.	The latter
has a slight lead at present, having won six

times to the former's five, one match being drawn.

Though I have but lightly touched on the development of this great game, it will be seen that each change that has been made has been in the direction of scientific and skilful play, as opposed to pure brute force. The public have recognized this, and so has the press. It is true that now and again a particularly pugnacious member of the " Peace Society," or some similar body, attacks the game in somewhat the same fashion as our friend Stubbes, describing it as little better than a " bloodie and murthering practice." Or it may be that a violent teetotaler declaims against it as encouraging thirst and improper language. But this is the exception, and not the rule. Such prejudice is the legacy left to us from the old days of hacking and tripping, to which, strange as it may seem, some elderly players still look back with an ill-concealed regret. Thus do the sins of our football fathers descend upon their children ; for the modern game is not brutal. To a certain extent it is dangerous ; but, then, what game is not ? Now and again a strong man loses his temper, or performs an act of retributive justice, and then some slight damage is done. I well remember a famous International recounting his experiences over his pipe on a winter's evening. "Once," he said, in a peculiarly solemn tone, "I was playing in Somerset against an up-country team, who were well known for their hard play. We had a little half, whose pluck was a great deal too big for his body, and one of their big wing forwards gave him a very poor time indeed. Well, I got hold of that big forward and I sent him outside the ropes." There was a pause, while the giant sent a cloud of smoke into the listening air. "What happened?" I queried. "I don't know," was the answer; "he didn't come back to tell me."

At the same time, serious accidents are of very rare occurrence. A sceptical person can discover that I do not simply speak as a mere football enthusiast by comparing the number of players with the number of accidents during the year. They will find the percentage extraordinarily small. The deaths from hunting, from skating, or from boating are infinitely more numerous, and yet faddists do not cry that we should never steer our way across a dangerous bit of country, or strap on our skates after a day's frost, or go for a row with a picnic party. A valuable bit of evidence is given us by that well-known American sportsman, Caspar Whitney. From his personal observation, he writes, " It comes to me that there is no ' slogging,' and their play is particularly free from ' roughing.' In all the games I witnessed, in not one did I see the slightest attempt at anything savouring of ' slogging.' Indeed, I am told the written and unwritten law on the subject is extremely severe, and that the transgressor would not only be ruled off the field for that game, but stand a good chance of being ruled off for the season. . . . Rugby Union is much freer of unnecessary roughness than our game as it is often played." It is pleasant to see ourselves as others see us, and to find we are regarded in so favourable a light. In America the keenness to win finds expression in the necessity for padded trousers, shin-guards, and head-protectors. It is not surprising to learn that in 1894 the Cambridge member of the Massachusetts State Legislature attempted to introduce a Bill providing for the punishment of one " who takes part in a game of football when such a game is played

in the presence of persons who have paid an
admission fee to witness the same, or who promotes
the playing of a game at football when money is
charged for admission to the same, or who offers
or sells a ticket of admission to the game, or who,
while a student in an institution of learning, and
while engaged in a game of football, beats, strikes,
or intentionally wounds or bruises another person
engaged in playing such a game." Such a Bill
has quite a flavour of mediæval England about
it, and would be improved by a few rounded
periods on the subject of the "beastlie furie,"
and the other disadvantages of this "devilishe
pastime."

However, in England at least Rugby football
has a secure position, and any changes that may
occur in it will not be in the direction of "slogging" or "roughing," as our kinsman terms rough
play. In the Universities, those most conservative
of institutions, it has got a firm hold. At first it
was regarded with considerable dislike. It was not
considered a gentlemanly amusement, though, in
connection with this, it must be remembered that
it was as late as the year 1837 that the Christ-
church crew at Oxford were requested to take

their boat off the river, although they were then
head of the summer eights, because the said
rowing was not a "gentlemanly amusement."
At a later date football aroused the hostility of
the boating men, for the strong and heavy athletes
who would make excellent "fours" and "fives"
in an eight were found "running about after a
piece of leather," as Cardinal Manning termed
the game. At Cambridge the opposition was so
strong that the boating men refused the football
players their "blue" — the distinguishing colour
which may only be worn by those who represent
their University in big athletic events. After a
great struggle, during which a great deal of bitter-
ness prevailed, the footballers, by a considerable
majority of the undergraduates assembled in the
Union Society's debating hall, were accorded the
right to wear the coveted coat of blue. At
Oxford the rowing men were more generous, and
granted the dark-blue coat as soon as it was seen
how popular the game was becoming, not only in
the Universities, but in England generally.

It would be easy to write many pages on the
advantages of the game, but it is unnecessary to
do so. The arguments in favour of athletics

will apply to Rugby football. It teaches a man
to keep his temper ; it gives a vent to that
desire, inherent in the Anglo-Saxon race, to
rejoice in some form of hard bodily exercise. It
was this feeling that sent the youths of a century
ago strolling round the town, boxing the watch
and collecting bell-handles as assiduously as the
most ardent philatelist collects rare specimens of
postage stamps. Again, it keeps young men out
of the bars, and, in this respect, is not only not
dangerous, but life-saving, for the drinking of bad
whisky is far worse than the breaking of a collar-
bone. Of course every game has its disadvantages,
and football is no exception to the rule. What
they are, and how they are bound up with the
question of professionalism, I will point out in the
next chapter, on the probable future of the game.

CHAPTER III.

THE FUTURE.

HE average prophet has not an enviable position. Partly it is his own fault. He always will insist on taking an extreme view of the future which passing events foreshadow. If he approves of the present, he is wildly optimistic as to the future ; if he objects to the direction in which matters seem tending, he cries aloud that everything is going to the dogs. When he makes the inevitable mistake, there is the inevitable candid friend—the worst of all enemies— on the watch to turn and rend him when he least expects it. If I now pose as a prophet, it is with due apology for the presumption. I will at least do my best to steer a middle course; I will try to avoid the necessity of "cutting" the candid friend.

Football, as I have already pointed out, began with the people. When we first meet it in history it was a people's game ; but for its first thirty years modern Rugby football was far more popular with the classes than with the masses. It came from the great public schools, and the first great clubs were composed almost entirely of young men from the upper and middle classes. Now, however, the game has been democratized again, and is, in the North especially, the great pastime of the labouring men. This is an excellent thing in many ways. It has softened the line dividing rank from rank ; it has shown the labourer that committees do not merely consider social position, but give the place in the team to the best player suited to the post, irrespective of who he may be. I remember an amusing incident taking place at Cambridge which is quite worth chronicling. A Cumberland team had come up to play the University. After the conclusion of the game one of the visiting forwards came up to a member of the county committee who had accompanied the team to Cambridge, and said, with an air of intense satisfaction, " When we coom oop to Cambridge, A was tebble

PASSING AMONGST THE FORWARDS

feared that they was nout but a set o' passons an'
that ; but t' fust mon as iver A git hod of, he
says to me, says he, 'Who the h—ll are you a-
collarin'?' A felt," said the worthy man, with a
placid smile of content on his face—" A felt nice
an' hoam-like after that."

Perhaps the best feature of this enthusiasm for
Rugby football which has grown up among
working men is the delight in hard exercise and
the consequent self-denial that it has taught them.
A man cannot spend his nights and his wages in
the public-house if twice a week he has to face
a hard struggle of forty minutes " each way." No
one is a keener sportsman than the true amateur
working-man football player. Many foreigners,
amongst whom the German Emperor stands conspicuous, have recognized the advantages of
artisan athletics. But it must be remembered
that they have an excellent substitute in their
military system. The few years of service, with
its gymnastic instruction, its route-marching, and
its general drilling, have a most favourable effect
on the national physique. We have, as is our
loudest boast—though why we should be so proud
of it it is difficult to understand—no compulsory

conscription. It seems probable that without such
games as football we should gradually sink from
our present *première* position in muscularity
amongst the European nations.

So far we have seen only the bright side of the
picture, but there is a dark side as well. For
a long time veiled professionalism has existed
amongst the working men in the North of England. The Rugby Union did what they could to
suppress it, but in vain. In 1895 the great
majority of Yorkshire and Lancashire clubs left
the Union, and formed a " Northern League " of
their own. At present they still claim the title
of " amateurs," but they have decided to pay
each man a sum of money for the loss of time
occasioned by his absence from his work.
Their arguments seem plausible enough. " Good
players," they say, " who belong to the labouring classes, are required to appear for their club
two or three times a week, and yet are expected
to lose their pay for the half-day without a murmur ; we only wish to remedy an injustice by
compensating them for the actual loss of wages
incurred." So far, perhaps, so good ; but the
Rugby Union knows, as well as do the Northern

clubs themselves, that this is but the thin edge of
the wedge. Once payments in hard cash are
publicly made, the regular wages of full professionalism will inevitably follow in time ; and "after
that—the deluge" for Rugby football in the North
of England.

The soil was ready for the sowing of the seed,
or rather, I should say, weed of professionalism.
Four or five years ago reports were in circulation
that certain players were regularly paid. A
standing joke against one well-known International, a University man, and one of the bitterest
opponents of professionalism, was, that after playing brilliantly for a certain Yorkshire club, he
returned to the pavilion to discover that his
enthusiastic admirers had deposited two pounds
fourteen shillings and eightpence in his boots !
His indignation can be better imagined than
described. Then, again, there was the extraordinary increase of gate - money, due to the
increased interest taken in the game. Great was
the temptation to an enthusiastic committee when
a fine three-quarter would declare his inability to
continue to play, either because he could get no
work, or because he could not afford to lose the

time, while at the same moment a good round sum was standing to their credit at their bankers. Further, the spectators, who supplied the sinews of war, began to be considered far more important than the sport itself. Regret would be expressed that a game was slow, or consisting of many scrummages, not because the players had not enjoyed themselves, but because " it had proved so uninteresting to the spectators." In other words, a match was turned into a theatrical entertainment, where the audience, having paid the money, expected to get good value for it. Betting, too, had made its appearance—betting which, as Mr. Rowland Hill terms it, is an " unmitigated curse to any branch of athletics it contaminates." Such was the situation when last year the Northern League broke from the Rugby Union, and declared its intention of sanctioning the payment of players for loss of time.

What will be the result of this change ? In the first place, there is no doubt that the whole of the clubs of the North of England will ultimately be drawn into the professional vortex. It is very discouraging to think of this fall of old clubs and old traditions. For many years Yorkshire and

Lancashire have produced the finest players, and, what is still more important, the most honourable sportsmen in England. But as club after club goes over to the great professional majority, the amateur must be squeezed out. At first he will join small amateur clubs, but as it becomes more and more difficult for him to play in matches with "foemen worthy of his steel," he will either cease to take an interest in football, or his play will deteriorate from the want of the practice which closely contested games alone afford. If there are any who do not believe this, let them look at the records of Association football in the North of England. From the moment professionalism appeared, amateurism declined, until there is not an amateur club, worthy of the name, between Berwick and Hull. But this is by no means the worst. I believe that the effect upon the game itself will be disastrous. In Association the hard-working rushing dribblers have disappeared; a complex machinery of tricky passes and "gallery" tactics has taken the place of the style of play followed by the man who turned out on the football field for the sake of good sport, fresh air, and healthy exercise. And Rugby is a very different

game from Association. It is more complex, to
begin with, and the very rules, despite the fact
that of late they have been made more stringent,
presuppose that each player is a sportsman
who looks rather to the spirit than the letter
of the law. During the last few years in those
clubs in which veiled professionalism was in existence, the players have studied the laws merely to
find loopholes for evasion. It was not until 1888
that penalties were inflicted for all serious forms of
foul play. At that time many of the old school of
Rugby footballers protested loudly. Let us, they
said, have no game at all if we cannot trust to the
sporting honour of the players. But penalties were
seen to be necessary, and what some matches
would now be like, if they were not in existence,
it is difficult to imagine. Let us listen to what
Mr. Montague Shearman says of professional
runners : " As soon as any sport has become so
popular that money is to be made out of it, and
men engage in it upon whom the loss of reputation
has little effect, it may be prophesied with certainty
that abuses will arise." This is not surprising. A
player who knows that he will have £5 in his
pocket if he wins the match, and only £2 if he

loses, is liable to find his sense of honour considerably dulled. It is but natural, after all, that
he who plays for money is ruled by commercial
instinct, while he who plays for sport is ruled by
the instincts of a sportsman. Then there is the
spectator. To draw big gates he must be considered. The play must be altered to suit his
tastes. Can anything be more objectionable?
The football players of the future will be compelled to forget the honourable traditions of this
great English game, and to pander to the howling
mob that crowd the circular stands of some Yorkshire Colosseum. Yet this is a movement encouraged by the Northern League. It has been
seriously proposed by them to alter the rules,
and reduce the number of players, in order that
the game may be faster and more "pleasing to
the spectators." I shrewdly suspect that, if the
truth be told, they hope, by knocking off two
forwards, to be able to save the weekly wages
they would otherwise be forced to pay them.
There is something to be said for their view of
the question. A travelling circus of fifteen men is
an expensive establishment to keep up.

In America we have an example of spectacular

football in full swing. In the great Inter-University
matches the "gate" is the first thing considered.
Not that the players are professionals, though a very
free hand is allowed them in expenses, but they
have become intoxicated with the interest taken in
them by the press and the public. For the benefit
of the curious, I will quote an account of a football match, played in 1893, between Princeton and
Yale colleges, published by a leading American
newspaper.   " Fifty thousand people," we are
told, "saw the great football game." The excitement was so great that, though "it may be maintained at the same point for many more seasons,
it cannot," writes the enthusiastic reporter, "pass
the point reached to-day, unless nature provides
humanity with more and wilder means of express-
ing excitement than were possessed by the mad
thousands that watched the game on Manhattan
field."   After some delay, "the excitement and
pent-up forces were turned loose in the usual way,
when a wildly agitated young man, clinging to the
top of a telegraph-pole over the dressing-rooms,
startled the stillness with a shriek, ' They're
coming ! ' The players appear.   Then for five
minutes there were wild indistinguishable cheers,

a tumult of horns and rattles, punctured by the far-
carrying blast of a trumpet sounding a martial
call. The twenty-two shock-headed youngsters"
(why, by-the-by, do American athletes wear their
hair so long? Is the fashion connected in any way
with the example set by Samson? It would be
interesting to discover) "ran out on the gridiron
and began cavorting round, as porpoises in the
water. Still there were deafening cheers. The
substitutes, coachers, doctors, and attendants
spread themselves out on blankets along the north
side line ; the captains were called up by the
umpire for a serious word of warning against
rough play, and at last play was called." What
a theatrical and tawdry business it all seems!
The spectators must be startled and interested.
Their enthusiasm must, if possible, be kept at
boiling point. The sport to be enjoyed sinks
away into mere nothingness. After the play has
started a player is hurt. "Blake got up and
Hinkey did not. He was insensible, and was
bleeding from a cut near the right ear. He was
taken off the field, protesting in a dazed manner,
and it was supposed that he was out of the game.
The substitutes ran on the field and blanketed the

players, who roamed about looking like Indians,
while every one waited anxiously for the news of
Hinkey. That intrepid and silent young man
reappeared after his injuries were bathed and
bandaged, and played out the game, looking gory
but game." When her line was broken, " Yale,"
we are told, " was dazed, Princeton was frantic.
Her substitutes fought the police in their efforts to
rush to their players." And so the report proceeds.

The American youths are undoubtedly plucky,
even to foolhardiness. I do not quarrel with
them there. What I dislike is this " improving
of the game," to speak in their own tongue, " off
the face of the earth." Their football is no longer
a sport ; it is an exhibition. " The outcome of the
contest," as one of their countrymen writes, " is
taken too seriously. The sight, familiar to us, of
members of a defeated football eleven throwing
themselves prostrate on the ground in an agony of
bitter disappointment, would, indeed, make Englishmen stare in wonderment." " The English idea
appears to be," says the same writer, " an afternoon's
sport first, and winning and records afterwards."
This is a great compliment. May we deserve it
as much in ten years time as we do to-day !

We may next inquire into what will result
from an alteration in the laws for the benefit of
the spectator. The game will be for the swift
of foot alone. Physique will be of little or no
consequence. The hard pushing in the scrummage, which broadened and straightened young
football players in the past, will disappear, and
with it will go the *raison d'être* of the game
in schools. Elderly football players have for
some time expressed strong opinions that the
"passing craze" is assuming absurd proportions.
I do not altogether hold with them there, but
I think it has gone about far enough. The
forwards are the majority and the backbone of a
Rugby football team. They must not become
mere heeling-out machines. The chief danger
of the professional spectacular game will be that
"the manly sport of football will degenerate into
the elegant art of catchball." It is true that,
as I have said, it will be most unsuitable for
schools, where doctors and head-masters agree
that the game is fast enough as it is. It is
also true that amateurs, who are in business all
the week, will find it impossible to maintain so
high a pitch of training as will be required if

they mean to compete with professionals. Yet,
after all, these are, so some think in the North,
mere matters of details not to be considered
for a moment while the public purse dangles
before the professional eye. Of one thing we
may be certain : the football of the future will
not be dangerous. With the same desire for
public approbation there will be none of the extraordinary keenness that characterizes American
football. To the professional mind a broken
collar-bone is scarcely an equitable exchange for
a month's wages. To deal out rough play means,
in all probability, to receive rough play. Thus it
will come about that the professional will become
mild in his gambols as the proverbial lamb, though
I have no doubt that in any technical disputes
he will roar him as loudly as the proverbial lion.

Before I close the chapter, I should like to
say a few words on professionalism from the stand-
point of those men who take the money. There
is nothing dishonourable in their so doing. In
fact, the foundation of the Northern League has
this advantage—that all the humbug of the semi-
amateurism that has existed for some time is done
away with. If professionalism must exist, it is

well for it to get up on a pedestal, and say what it
has to say for itself, and not slink about in holes and
corners. Mr. Montague Shearman read the signs
of the times correctly several years ago, when
he declared that payment of players must come, and
that the legislation of the Rugby Union was only
driving professionalism beneath the surface. He
concluded, however, that it would not seriously
injure the game, and called the professional
cricketer to witness that he spoke correctly. I
entirely differ from him there. I have said
that I believe that the effect of it upon the style
of play will be most injurious. Now I will go
further, and say that its effect upon the professionals themselves will be equally harmful. In
cricket there is a constant demand for champions who have passed their prime as groundmen,
bowlers at the nets, and umpires. But there will
be no such chances of employment for elderly
Rugby football professionals. If the Northern
League can carry out its pledges, and pays for
broken time alone, encouraging the players to
continue their work in the mills for the rest of
the week, all may be well. But the question
is, Can they do it? If the Rugby professional

system is to be modelled on that practised by
the Association clubs, and men are bought by
one club from another, so that the richest club
may have the best team, while the players give
up their old employments to depend on football
alone, then, I say, the position of those men
will be most precarious. Fifteen men are a large
number to support, and it is doubtful if, as a
spectacle, Rugby football will attract the immense
crowds that flock to the Association matches. If
clubs get into difficulties, and if there are hints
that players, like rowing, running, and wrestling
professionals in the past, have taken bribes, the
public support will melt away, and they will find
themselves without a trade and without means of
support. Yet, again, the football life of a man is
but short, as compared to his cricketing life. At
twenty-eight or nine he is getting stiff, and Rugby
football of all games requires suppleness and
activity. In his ten years of play he will have
forgotten his trade, and grown accustomed to a
better style of living than his position warranted.
What will then become of him? It is not a
particularly pleasant thought to dwell upon.

I will quote a couple of extracts on the

subject from Mr. Whitney, whose work I have
already had occasion to mention. "What," he
asks, "has the professional done for Association
football in return for having taken it into the fold?
He has given it a great popularity among his kind,
a popularity which, like a flash in the pan, will die
away as quickly as it flamed, once deprived of
artificial kindling. . . . He has, in fine, vitiated
the football atmosphere of the British Kingdom."
There is no doubt as to what is our American
friend's opinion. He hits out straight from the
shoulder. He is an authority too; for, during his
stay, he inquired into every detail of English
sport in the most painstaking manner possible.
Listen to what he says on the whole subject: "It
is absolutely true that whenever or wherever an
element enters sport for profit, corruption is certain
to follow. Will any one tell me of one game
which professionals have dominated that has not,
starting out with a boom, ended in final decay after
a life of corruption and scandal? How runs the
history of professional foot-racing, boating, and
pugilism?" Right again, Mr. Whitney! Professional "peds," as they were called, were discovered to be so hopelessly corrupt, that the class

to which they belonged became a bye-word amongst sportsmen ; professional boating is practically dead ; while pugilists are for the most part members of our colonies, who come over to box for the purses we provide. Wrestling, too, he might have added ; for many of its meetings have been abandoned owing to the discovery that the champions divided the prizes before they stripped for the struggle. It was only due to its great amateur strongholds at Oxford and Cambridge, that boating was not entirely "dominated" by professionalism. Running, for the same reason, partially escaped its fell clutches. When at last the public rose in its wrath and swept away the mass of corruption which clustered round these great sports, the amateur emerged stronger and healthier for what had been done. But if the whole of the North of England goes over to professional Rugby football, and the imported player, as is invariably the case, stamps out what local talent exists, then the game will have been entirely "dominated" by professionalism. When the time comes for the "roping" and "pulling," and the shady tricks that appear with a decline of gate-money and a lack of wages for the performers ;

when at last the public shakes the football circus
from its shoulders,—then it will be found that
Rugby football is dead in those districts where
the professional flourished. It will have grown in
bad odour, amateurs will have given up the game
in disgust, and when, in the end, the professional
goes, as go he must, Rugby football will disappear
with him.

What can an amateur do to stem the tide?
Little enough—as far as I can see. Time alone
can satisfactorily solve the problem of professionalism. At the same time, he can set his face
sternly against the slightest suspicion of pseudo-
amateurism. Let him play the game for the sake
of the game, and not of the spectators ; let him
be most scrupulous in his dealings with gate-
money. The amateur may fairly take money
for the railway and hotel expenses which he
incurs. It would be impossible otherwise for a
man, not too well blessed with this world's
goods, to travel about the country with his club.
I remember that when this very subject was
under discussion in a Cambridge newspaper, a
smart epigram appeared which is well worth
quoting—

E

" You ask me whether 'tis to be commended
   To take from out the gate enough to meet
What you in football tourings have expended.
   Well, what did Samson, prototype athlete,
At Gaza? Some, of course, of what he then did
   You may omit ; but mark how, when he beat
The Philistines, he did not hesitate,
But made his exit, *taking all the gate.*"

Our amateurs must not, however, be so extortionate in their demands. If they follow the example of the " prototype athlete " too far, they will find a Delilah, in professional football, who will cut their combs with a vengeance. Big dinners, champagne, cigars, must come out of their own pockets, or they will soon find that they will be unable to cast out the motes from the professional eye by reason of the beams in their own. It may seem that I have painted the picture in sombre tints ; but I think that the majority of football players will agree that I have not exaggerated the dangers that threaten Rugby football in the future. If I have done so, I most humbly apologize. *Absit omen !*

CHAPTER IV.

FORWARD PLAY.

By Frank Mitchell,

Captain Cambridge XV., 1895 ; Captain England *v.* Scotland, 1896.

OF STYLES OF PLAY.

I SHOULD imagine that there is nobody caring much about football that has not enjoyed "Tom Brown's Schooldays." Readers will doubtless remember how at Rugby the greater part of the players spent their time shoving in the scrummage. The forwards bore the burden and heat of the fray ; and, in spite of altered tactics and altered rules, this may as truthfully be said of the modern forwards as of those of an earlier day. Of course they do the work in a different manner ; but they have to do it all the same.

Several styles of play have been in vogue since the game began. The scrummage has not been excepted from this evolution, and even now forward play may still be said to be imperfect. When a team consisted of twenty players a side, as it did in the sixties and early seventies, some fourteen of that number (I speak without authority) were in the scrummage, and formed a large and compact mass, from which the ball seldom emerged. Nowadays, when eight forwards a side is the recognized number, it often happens that the scrummage is no sooner formed than it is broken up again. Old players amongst us are fond of relating the Homeric conflicts between the opposing forwards when a scrummage lasted for five minutes, and one side gained the mastery by straight, hard shoving. The end and object of a forward's life was to shove straight ahead, oblivious of the position of the ball, until the other side was worn down before his and his companions' efforts. Under such circumstances it is easy to imagine that there was very little room for any skill which was not backed by a large quantity of muscle. Of course there is no doubt that at that period there were some very fine

players of the "bull-dog" type; but I venture
to state that did those players exist now, they
would either be completely run off their legs
or would have to entirely alter their style of
play.

In later times, when nine forwards and three
three-quarters were played, the game of the
forwards, though it may seem very reactionary to
say so, was almost an ideal one. They were not,
as we sometimes find them now, mere machines to
get the ball for their backs to do the work with,
but they were allowed to take their fair share of
the game both in attack and defence. In the
present day of four three-quarters, there are still
several styles of forward play quite distinct from
one another. Firstly, there is the Welsh style,
which, being interpreted, means that the chief duty
of a forward is to play for the benefit of his backs.
Secondly, we have the Scotch style, which many
call the old style. No doubt it bears a greater
resemblance to the play in vogue in the early
eighties than any other of the present systems.
Then we have, thirdly, the Yorkshire style, which
is the kick-and-rush game. Lastly, we have the
Southern and University style, which cannot be

said to resemble the play of either the Welshmen, Scotchmen, or Yorkshiremen.

In the Welsh game there is practically no footwork. In Scotland, on the contrary, every club has forwards who dribble splendidly, and in this accomplishment they have dangerous rivals in the Irishmen. An ideal style would be that which combined the energy and footwork of the Scotch with the neatness and passing power of the Welsh. In time, I have little doubt that such a style will be in vogue in the great clubs in the South of England.

Forward play may be roughly divided under the following heads :—Scrummage play, dribbling, tackling, following up, touch play, and kicking.

Scrummage Play.

First, then, let us deal with the play in the scrummage, which, all things considered, is by far the most important part of the forward game. I think that the first thing which is impressed on the majority of school forwards is to remember, on entering a scrummage, that their duty is to shove hard and to watch the ball. If all forwards paid attention to these two rules, how much higher would be the general average of the play in the present day!

Now, as to the formation of a scrummage. With eight forwards—the usual number nowadays —the best plan would appear to be to have three in the front row. To this there is one exception. When near the goal-line of the enemy, let four place themselves in the front row, for by this arrangement it will be easier to heel the ball out to the halves, and, in addition, the front row will be able to hold back the sides of the opposing scrummage from rushing on to the halves, and preventing their passing the ball when they do receive it. When packing for the scrummage, no loose spaces should be left; and the front rank should take great care that their opponents do not get under them, for they will thereby lose half their shoving power. It is like the undergrip in a wrestle.

When the scrummage is packed, the possession of the ball is the next thing to be thought of, and the front rank should try to obtain it by getting the first shove. There must be no standing on one leg while attempts are made to hook the ball back with the other. While forwards are trying to do this, the other side, if worth their salt, will shove them back, and thus be able to take possession of the ball. If your forwards have got the first shove and the ball, the rest is comparatively easy. The ball is now carefully stowed away in the second rank—not further back—and the plan of attack must at once be decided. If the ball is to be shoved straight through, honest hard work alone will succeed. Every man must work "all he knows." If, on the other hand, the idea is to screw the scrummage, the word must be given, and the front rank at once must commence to shove in the opposite direction to which the ball is to go. By this they are able to push their opponents off the ball, and leave the way clear for the remaining five who have the ball in their possession. The front three thus act as a screen, behind which the five can develop the attack. When the five have started off with the ball, the remaining three should whip round and fall into the rear rank. Every one should carefully watch the ball throughout, and be always ready to use their feet to steer the ball to one side or the other, as may be directed by the captain.

Perhaps diagrams will better explain what I mean to those who know but little about the game.

SCREWING THE SCRUMMAGE.

In the first diagram we see an ordinary scrummage. The A forwards obtain the first shove, and, pushing the B forwards back, obtain the ball, which is stowed away in their second row, which is underlined. In the second diagram we see the front row of the A forwards pushing in the direction of the arrow, and sliding off the B forwards from

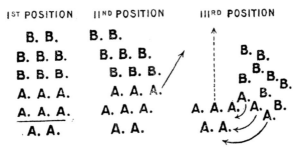

the second and third rank of the A forwards. In the third diagram we find the B forwards disorganized by finding the A scrummage melt away before them, while the second and third row of the A forwards are off with the ball in the direction of the dotted line ; their first row now falls in behind them, as shown by the curling arrows, leaving the B forwards floundering after them.

DRIBBLING.

We now find our forwards, having successfully screwed the scrummage, ready for a rush to the enemy's goal-line. It is absolutely necessary that they should be able to dribble. The lack of foot-work and of men who can dribble fairly well amongst the English clubs is most surprising. It is true that to dribble a Rugby ball while running fast is a matter of no little difficulty, but with practice there is absolutely no reason why every player should not become fairly efficient. Boys should be taught to dribble well at school. At the Universities players have plenty of opportunities for practice, and in the majority of clubs they could, if they choose, put in a quarter of an hour's fast dribbling of an evening, which will keep them up to the proper standard. As they make the rush, the forwards should spread out like a fan, and pass with their feet—after the manner of the players of the Association game—each player, however, taking great care to keep behind the man dribbling, and thus "on side." When passing a ball in this manner the young player will find it more easy

to use the outside of the foot than the inside. On
nearing the enemy's goal-line, the ball, if bouncing
about knee height, should be picked up, and the
passing amongst the forwards be continued by
hand instead of by foot. The ball should not be
kicked over the line if it is possible to avoid
so doing. Kicking the ball over the line in Rugby
is practically the same as kicking it out of play
in Association ; for it is ten to one that some
one amongst the opposing side touches it down.

TACKLING.

In the open a forward should always tackle
low and hard. But when at close quarters, as
at the touch-line, it will be found much better
to take a man round the shoulders. The neck
looks very tempting under these circumstances,
but my advice is leave it alone, and go for the
shoulders. Tackling by the neck, or "scragging,"
as it is often called, may lead to an accident,
and is almost certain to produce some ill-feeling
which, it is hardly necessary for me to say, should
be avoided at all costs. A forward should be
always ready to come to the assistance of his

backs by running after a man and tackling him.
He will find that, if he breaks out of the scrummage as soon as the ball emerges from it, he will
often be able to double across the field in time
to be of valuable assistance in breaking up one
of those machine-like pieces of passing so much
in vogue at the present time. There is always
a chance that the man he is pursuing may be
turned by another player, and that he may be able
to catch him up and tackle him.

FOLLOWING UP.

Another important part of a forward's duty
consists in "following up." A forward must
follow up every kick—whether it be kick-off,
drop-out, or free kick—as hard as he can run.
There must be no slacking, no waiting for the
opposing three-quarters to return the ball if it has
not found touch. He must set off at top speed,
converging slightly, but not too much, towards
the point where the ball will fall. If two or three
forwards come charging down on a back at the
same moment, he will evade them—if at all—with
the greatest difficulty. On the other hand, it is

the simplest thing in the world to dodge a single
man running at top speed. When a forward sees
that his own backs are off with the ball, he should
follow up hard, so that he may be at hand to take
a pass. The same rule applies in the case of a
single player breaking away with the ball from a
line-out ; he should never be unsupported.

The Northern forwards can teach the South-
erners a tremendous amount in following up hard,
though it must be confessed that they do not
always keep on-side when so doing. The muddy
state of the grounds on which the Northern teams
play renders it impossible for the backs to be sure
of catching the ball, and gives many more opportunities to those energetic forwards who have
followed up hard, and who are upon the backs
before they can recapture the ball should it be
fumbled by them. A great deal may be done,
wet or fine, by keen following up ; a player often
finds that the opposing three-quarter has missed
the ball, and that he has it in his possession with
only the back to pass before the goal is reached.
In moments like this he will fully appreciate the
rich reward of keen " following up."

Touch Play.

This feature of the game, which I consider one of the most interesting, has been most seriously attacked during the past two seasons, and indeed threatened with extermination. There are very few hints to be given as to how to get the ball, but it is quite easy to prevent the other side from getting it. Let everybody, in the first instance, mark his man. The best players generally seem to jump up to catch the ball, and some, as Lohden of Blackheath, can catch it in one hand, and with the other ward off his *vis-à-vis* as he tries to tackle him. This style of play is not, however, recommended to the notice of those who take less than nines in their glove measure. If a player gets through the line, he should be ready to give a pass, and this should, as a general rule, be given on the open side of play.

Kicking.

I have now dealt with those duties of a forward which are generally considered to be of most importance. But beyond these a forward should

make a point of practising kicking and catching
the ball. Two or three forwards are nowadays
always deputed to. stand back at the kick-off to
catch and return short kicks. A slight error on
their part, either in the catching or in the kicking, may easily turn into a serious blunder,
materially affecting the fortunes of the contest.
Moreover, if a forward is a safe kick, a sure catch,
and a hard tackle, he becomes of additional value
to his side, for he can be called out of the scrummage either if one of the three-quarters is injured,
or if the goal-line is threatened, and a helping
hand amongst the backs is needed. In fact, at
the present time, a forward to be really of the
first rank should not only be able to do the heavy
cart-horse work of the scrummage, but also be
prepared, at a moment's notice, to undertake the
lighter and more skilful work of an outside.

A few words as to place-kicking—that much-
neglected branch of the game—may be of use,
although little can be said which will teach players
to become really proficient. Constant practice
is the secret of success in place-kicking. If
possible, always get the same man to place the
ball for you. When a try has been obtained

between the posts, or but a yard or two outside
them, so that the kick at goal is a short one, I
should advise a player to have the ball placed
straight up like an egg on end. For longer

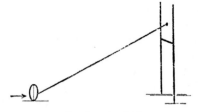

1. For close place-kick.

2. For long place-kick.

distances have the ball placed with the lace upper-
most leaning towards the goal, so that a line
drawn through the centre of the ball would pass

over the centre of the cross-bar. To explain my
meaning more fully, I have given a diagram (p. 80).

Finally—and this is the most important thing
of all—never take your eyes off the ball as you run
to kick it. Watch the ball from the moment you
start to the moment you kick. To look at the
goal or anywhere else is as fatal in place-kicking
as it would be in driving at golf or playing a ball
at cricket. The run for the longest kick should
not be more than from six to seven yards.

GENERAL REMARKS.

Perhaps it might be of some interest to the
readers of this book if I tried to enumerate some
of the most distinguished forwards of the past few
years. As to all-round forwards, the best of recent
date have undoubtedly been W. E. Bromet, R. G.
MacMillan, and T. Cream. All these men are exceedingly strong, fast, and clever; able both in the
tight and in the loose to display their powers to
great advantage. Next to them I should place C.
B. Nicholl, W. McEwen, G. T. Neilson, J. O'Conor,
T. Broadley, W. E. Tucker, and G. M. Carey. All
these men are sterling workers, and are never found
far from the ball, wherever it may be. Perhaps

F

the best scrummage-player I ever saw was W.
Yiend. I firmly believe that he would be able to
shove any two players of the present day. The
amount of work he managed to get through was
simply enormous. R. D. Budworth, C. V. Rooke,
L. F. Giblin, and A. W. Boucher are the best " out
of touch " men of my time. At the wing game
none have ever been the equal of Sam Woods
and F. Evershed. The best forward teams in my
football experience have been those that represented
Newport in 1892, Ireland in 1894, and Scotland in
1896. And here may I be pardoned if I state
that, in my opinion, the Cambridge forwards of
the Christmas term of 1895 were as powerful as
any of late years, though perhaps not quite so
dashing as some of the other teams that I have
mentioned.

The ideal weight for a forward is thirteen stone,
and five feet ten inches is, I should say, the ideal
height. A captain should, in picking his team,
try, as far as possible, to get together forwards of
the same size. They will pack far better in the
scrummage than a mixed lot of varying statures.
Let him, as I have already stated, remember to
have one or more men that he can call out of the
scrummage if necessary. It is sometimes good

policy for him to have out a forward in his own twenty-five, especially if he finds that his forwards can hold their opponents.

Finally, as a forward should never slack or "take a rest" for a single instant during the game, it is absolutely necessary that he should get into condition and keep fit throughout the season. "Early to bed and early to rise" should be his motto. A pair of Indian clubs swung for half an hour a day will do a great deal towards keeping the muscles in working order. Further, he should, if possible, take a daily run with the ball, and also practise dribbling. And here I should like to enter a protest against the use of heavy dumb-bells. They only stiffen the muscles, and do not impart any of that elasticity which is so necessary for a player. A famous member of bygone English teams once told me that he has for many years regularly used the clubs for an hour every day. Even as late as the last International match at Glasgow he was anxious to wager that he could swing them for an hour without stopping! And he must be nearly forty years old. May all the forwards of the present day be able to make such a challenge when they have advanced well into the next century!

CHAPTER V.

HALF-BACK PLAY.

By R. H. Cattell,

Oxford University and English International.

SINCE the sixties, when Rugby football first became a recognized game, its history has been a history of change. Each development has been in the direction of greater speed and great skill. The rules that govern the game, and the position and number of the players have been altered from time to time. From these alterations the style of half-back play has not been excepted. At first the half-back was by far the most important member of the back division. He did nearly all the running and most of the tackling. He never thought of any one but himself. Passing was unheard of, being considered practically equivalent to "funking." Everything in the nature of "gallery" play was entrusted to him. But when the number of players was diminished, and forwards no longer stuck in the scrummage, oblivious of what was going on around them, the half-back had of necessity to change his methods.

It was not, however, till 1881 that J. Payne started the system of passing the ball out to the three-quarters. He was followed by A. Rotherham, who absolutely revolutionized half-back play. It was he who demonstrated that a half-back should not play for himself alone, and that he is, before anything else, a link between the scrummage and the three-quarters. He showed, too, what valuable assistance a half could render to the three-quarters by affording openings for them. "Rotherham's game" was, and is, a household word in the great Rugby football family.

During the last four or five years the style of half-back play has again changed, though not to such a great extent as in the time of Rotherham. This was brought about by the introduction of four three-quarters, and the consequent reduction of the number of forwards to eight, an alteration which tended to make the game still faster, and so more tiring to the half-back. There are so many different opinions about modern half-back play, that I feel that whatever any individual writes about it is almost sure to meet with a certain amount of adverse criticism. However, this is only to be expected, when it is remembered that the game has developed, and is still developing.

The position of half-back always seems to me to be the most difficult of any on the field to fill satisfactorily. Its importance is immense, for the efficacy of the three-quarters depends almost entirely on the play of the half-backs. Yet in no position is commendation so rarely bestowed. In the old days of football amongst the Yorkshire operatives, there was a general rule of "When in doubt, mob the referee." So with a great many football teams there is a habit that may be summed up in similar words, as, "When you play badly, blame the halves." When forwards are being rushed, and three-quarters will not take passes, the lot of the half, like that of the policeman in Mr. Gilbert's song, "is not a happy one."

THE QUALIFICATIONS NECESSARY.

The most necessary qualifications for a half-back
are quickness, unselfishness, and pluck. At the
same time a certain amount of weight is a great
advantage; for behind losing forwards the half-
back has a very hard time indeed. There is a
tendency to play half-backs too light. A light
man often has exactly the quickness and activity
required, yet, with certain brilliant exceptions, he
cannot stand the wear and tear of hard defensive
play. It is most important that there should be
perfect understanding between the two halves.
Two moderate players who thoroughly understand
each other's game, will frequently score off two
first-class men who are playing together for the
first time. By the introduction of bye-play, and
those tricks which experience has shown to be the
most effective, they are able to entirely bewilder
opponents who, though individually superior, are
yet strangers to each other and lacking in the
necessary combination. Combination is the oil
which allows the passing machine to work smoothly
behind the scrummage.

The Attacking Game.

As the attacking game is the most important for winning matches, it will be best to discuss a half-back's play under these conditions first. Perhaps I can make my meaning clearer by appending a diagram of the system I am about to describe.

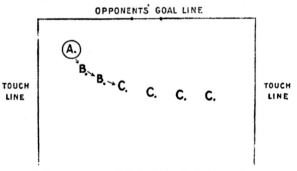

A, the scrummage ; B, B, the half-backs ; C, C, C, C, the three-quarters ; → direction of the ball.

Now, when the ball is in the scrummage near the opponents' goal-line, the forwards will, if they know their business, try and obtain the ball and heel it out sharply and cleanly. The first half-back should "work" the scrummage ; that is to

A SCRUMMAGE

say, he should stand about two yards behind it in
such a position that he may pick up the ball and
pass it to his partner the moment it emerges. The
second half-back should fall back some eight or
nine yards, and be ready to receive the ball from
his partner, and then either run himself or pass
it on to his three-quarters as opportunity offers.
The pass from the first to the second half-back
must be made in one motion, the ball being
swept off the ground and thrown hard and low
about the height of the thighs. The half-back
who is "working" the scrummage must not stand
too near to it ; for should the ball be heeled out
swiftly, it may go between his legs before he has
time to stop it. To have to turn round and run
after it is fatal, for the opposing half will, in all
probability, reach it as soon as he does himself.
There are several other risks which are run by
standing too close to the scrummage. A half, for
example, may find himself penalized for picking
the ball out from amongst the legs of his forwards,
or, worse still, he may get badly kicked in the
face by some enthusiastic heeler-out in the back of
the scrummage—an accident which once occurred
to the writer, and resulted in a severe black eye.

The half "working" the scrummage should rarely try to run himself. Good opponents will never leave him unmarked. He must also remember that there is another half and four three-quarters waiting for the ball, who are put there for the purpose of scoring tries. The half that is standing back may, if he finds himself unmarked, run himself, as he will then be able to slip through the line of opposing three-quarters, and have only the full back to dodge. If this manœuvre is tried, his partner must take care to back him up closely, that he may find a friend to whom he may pass should the full back seem able to tackle him. But if, as is usually the case, he finds himself watched too closely, he must hand on the ball as quickly as he can to the nearest three-quarter. A half should remember two other points which are of extreme importance. He must always see exactly where he is going to send the ball before he throws it. A wild pass is terribly risky. His opponents may secure the ball while his three-quarter is fumbling with it, and thus put a very different complexion on the game. He must, as the second point, make a rule never under any circumstances to pass the ball over his head, or, in other words, raise the ball over his head, and then throw it while in that position. The result is, nine times out of ten, that the ball falls at the feet of the three-quarter to whom it is sent, and it thus becomes practically impossible for him to secure it. This method of passing has the further disadvantage that, when the ball is despatched from such a high level, it may be easily intercepted by an opposing three-quarter, who rushes in to seize it. Let him therefore throw it hard and low with an underhand sweep, and, as I have said, let it reach the three-quarter to whom it is directed at the level of his thighs or waist.

When very near the opponents' goal-line a timely dash by a fast half-back will often result in a score, when a pass back to the three-quarters would only lose ground. A man must of course rely on his own judgment in such matters. At the same time, I will give the plan (p. 92) of a combination between the halves that may be tried once or twice during a game when close to the goal-line of the enemy.

Here the second half-back, instead of retiring eight or nine yards back from the first half-back, who is taking the scrummage, stands nearer to

him, and between him and the touch-line, instead
of outside of him, as shown in my first diagram.
When the first half-back gets the ball he gives it
to the second, who dashes in, keeping close to the
touch-line.   It is a smart piece of play, but should
not be tried too often, as it is useless if the other
side are on the look out for it.

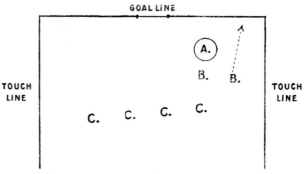

A, the scrummage ; B, B, the half-backs ; C, C, C, C, the three-
quarters ; – – – –➔ path of half-back.

As an example of modern offensive play I think
I may say, without fear of contradiction, that that
of C. M. Wells, the late Cambridge half-back and
English International, is the most brilliant and in
every way worthy of being copied.

DEFENSIVE PLAY.

The hardest part of a half-back's duties consists
in defensive play. Defensive play to a half-back
generally means either stopping the rushes of the
forwards of the opposing team after they have
routed the forwards on his own side, or else watching the opposing halves to see that they do not
get away with or pass the ball when it is heeled
out of the scrummage to them. Stopping forward
rushes is a most unpleasant performance, and it is
hardly necessary to say that, like many other disagreeable duties, it is often " more honoured in the
breach than the observance." Yet a half-back will
never be worth his salt until he can do what in
football language is known as "donkey work." It
is a very important part of the game, and every
half-back should pay particular attention to it, for
an inferior team has often been known to stave off
defeat by the persistent efforts of its halves, and
eventually win by a dropped or a penalty goal.
A half can only stop the rushes of the opposing
forwards by throwing himself on the ball. Never,
under any circumstance, must he try to stop the
ball with his foot, as he is naturally tempted to

do. He may miss it, he may be pushed out of the way, he may kick it straight into the hands of an opposing three-quarter ; in a word, a flying kick is to be strictly avoided by all good halves, for the chances against its success are about three to one.

It certainly sounds both difficult and dangerous to throw one's self on the ball at the feet of eight burly forwards, but if it be done as the scrummage is breaking up and before they get their pace up in the open it is fairly easy, and the risk of a bad kick is but slight. I should advise a half to read the hints given by C. J. N. Fleming in his chapter on " Three-quarter-Back Play " in the present book. He points out the danger of falling " head on " to the feet of the advancing forwards, and suggests that the best method is that of falling as much as possible away from them, so that the back and hips are turned towards them. But there must be no hesitation and no funk. Funk is the cause of the majority of accidents just as much in football as in hunting or mountaineering. " He who hesitates is lost," is a safe maxim for Rugby football.

Of the players of the present day, W. P. Donaldson, the Scotch International, gives the

best exposition of stubborn defensive play, and it
requires a brilliant set of forwards to keep the ball
out of his embrace.

I will now speak of the position of the halves
when the opposing forwards have obtained possession of the ball in the scrummage, and are
trying to heel it out to their own halves, who are
waiting to receive it in the manner I have already
described in my remarks on the attacking game.
Perhaps I had again better give a plan that will
illustrate my meaning.

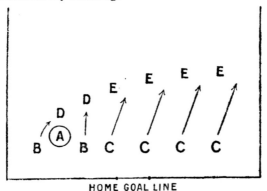

HOME GOAL LINE

A, the scrummage ; B, B, half-backs ; C, C, C, C, three-quarters ;
  D, D, attacking half-backs ; E, E, E, E, attacking three-
  quarters ; →, →, lines in which players must run upon D
  getting the ball.

Under these circumstances the home halves,
B, B, must follow the ball round the scrummages
as they see it being passed backwards by the heels
of the attacking forwards. They must not, according to the latest rules, get in front of it or hamper
the attacking half who is "working the scrummage" before he has the ball ; but immediately
it comes out of the scrummage they must make a
rush for it, and try either to secure it themselves,
or so hamper the attacking half-back who is
"working" the scrummage that he cannot pass it
to his companion. If he is able to pass it, they
must run on and help their own three-quarters to
tackle their opponents. The arrow lines I have
drawn will show the right movements that must
be made by the home half-backs and three-quarters
the moment the ball is seen to be in the hands
of their opponents.

One of the elementary rules drummed into boys
at school is that they must never pass the ball in
their own twenty-five, for fear of the pass being
intercepted or some miscatch made that would
give the ball to the enemy. This style of play is
nevertheless practised by the Welsh players with
some success. Yet it is so extremely dangerous that

the rule should never be broken by any one who
is less skilful at passing than are the Welshmen.
On the contrary, if the half gets possession of the
ball in his own twenty-five he should always try to
punt into touch. He must be careful not to punt
into the open field, or he may present his opponents
with a dropped goal. It is thus absolutely necessary that he should be able to punt well with
either foot. Nothing disheartens attacking forwards
so much as a good punt into touch, which regains
the ground they have worked so hard to win.
This was particularly noticeable in the England *v.*
Scotland match of 1895, when the punting into
touch by the Scotch halves went a long way
towards the victory of their side.

Throwing out of Touch.

Another duty falls to the half-back which I
wish to mention, namely, throwing the ball in from
the touch-line. Some teams adopt the plan of
each forward taking a particular place in the line-
out, but I do not think this advisable. The half-
back should have a good look to see where his
best forwards are standing, and then try to drop

G

the ball into their hands.   Some forwards are well
known for their good play in the line-out, amongst
whom I should mention S. M. J. Woods, of
England, and C. B. Nicholl, of Wales.   Players
who are famous for their skill in this branch of
the game adopt two methods.   The one consists
in standing slightly back from the line of men,
and when the ball is dropped by a knowing half-
back just opposite to where they are standing, they
come at it with a rush that takes them through
the opposing line of forwards.   The other consists
in simply taking the ball in an ordinary manner,
and then either ducking their heads and bolting
under the arms of their *vis-à-vis,* or attempting to
slip past him in the best way possible.   It is
thus sufficiently obvious that the art of throwing
in the ball from the line-out should be made the
subject of careful study by every half-back.   As
in everything else, proficiency can only come by
practice, and to that I recommend him.

    Another important point must be mentioned,
although it has probably been known to every
half-back since he first arrayed himself in his
school jersey.   When his own goal-line is threatened, he must throw the ball but a short distance

A THROW OUT OF TOUCH

into the field; when, on the contrary, he belongs to the attacking side, he should, subject to certain circumstances above mentioned with regard to the position of the players, throw it as far out as possible. For this the reason is obvious. By sending the ball into the middle of the field he affords an opportunity for loose play amongst the forwards and three-quarters, and also makes it probable that, if a try is to be obtained, it will be obtained in an advantageous position for kicking a goal. To throw the ball far out when near his own goal-line is simply suicidal. Much ground may sometimes be gained at the throw-out from touch by a combination between a half and a forward who know each other's play. Thus a half may throw the ball to a forward near the touch-line, who thereupon turns his back on the opponent who is marking him and passes the ball again to the half, who has by this time run from the touch-line to receive it. The forward may be tackled, but if he is big and strong it is hard for his opponent to prevent the pass. The half, when he obtains the ball, can either pass to a three-quarter, or slip through the line, or, best of all, kick into touch further down the touch-line.

Of course it is not meant that a half should always adopt the same tactics, for the more he varies them the more completely will he " bluff " his *vis-à-vis*. Some half-backs seem to have a natural genius for the game, and can see at a glance what combinations are likely to prove successful ; some, on the other hand, do not possess this gift, and then they must watch and attempt to imitate those who are more fortunate in this respect than they are themselves.

CHAPTER VI.

THREE-QUARTER-BACK PLAY.

By C. J. N. Fleming,

Captain of Oxford University, 1890.

IN writing of three-quarter-back play, I may safely assume that in the vast majority of clubs four three-quarters are played, although the old style of three still lingers in Scotland. As a matter of fact, it does not make much difference whether three or four are played, for the style of game is practically the same. Of course the four three-quarter game is the more difficult, owing to its complexity ; but a really good player is good either as one of three or one of four. Nor does it make much difference whether a player is on the wing or in the centre, for a good player ought at

once to adapt himself to his position. The first
essential in a three-quarter is that he should be a
good defensive player. This is a point which is
often overlooked, for people seem satisfied with
players who may be brilliant try-getters, but
whose defensive play is very weak. This, I feel
certain, is wrong, and there is no reason why a
player should not be equally practised in both
departments. For defence, a player must kick,
must save, and must tackle.

KICKING.

As for kicking, there are not many hints to be
given ; it can only be learnt by practice. A
player must learn to be a safe catch and safe
field, and then learn to kick quickly. Drop-
kicking is, I am sorry to say, rather at a discount
nowadays ; for unless a player is a very sure kick,
dropping at goal does not pay. When further
a-field, a punt is probably more accurate, can be
kicked rather quicker, and is just as effective. At
the same time, young players should practice
dropping assiduously ; for if a player can drop-
kick well, he will always get innumerable chances

of making good use of this art. In punting, the first thing to learn is to punt the ball to a particular spot. This is not hard in practice ; but, of course, in a game it is not easy to accurately land your kick in touch at the right place.

But kicking into touch, though the simplest form of kicking and perhaps commonest, is by no means the most important. Judicious kicking for following up is really the highest form of the art. In kicking for following up, the idea is to kick the ball in such a way that it will reach the ground just as the kicker, or some one else on the kicker's side who was not off-side when the kick was made, arrives there, and either appropriates the ball himself or prevents an opponent from returning the kick. When playing against a strong wind this usually proves most effective ; down wind, too, when a back finds himself close to his own goal a high kick into the field well followed up will prove a good way of clearing his lines.

Then, again, there are short kicks just over an opponent's head. Take, for instance, the case of a player coming straight at a full back, unsupported by any one to whom he may pass. In such an emergency the runner may punt the ball

just over the back's head, catch it again either on
the bound or else before it touches the ground,
and go straight in and obtain a try without
slackening his pace. It is almost impossible for a
back to stop a man under these conditions, but it
is an extremely difficult bit of play. To learn it,
a player should constantly practise giving small
punts straight in front of him, following up and
trying to catch them. As a variant of this
manœuvre, a player should study the trick of kicking across to one of his own side. Thus suppose he
is well away, but is blocked in front, or is afraid to
pass through fear of having his pass intercepted ;
he should then kick across in front of his own
forwards, but taking care that the ball flies over
the heads of his opponents, so that one of his
own side may dash forward and secure it. His
opponents are helpless, for they have no time to
turn round and get the ball themselves. To
better explain my meaning, I will give a diagram
of the field of play (p. 105).

I mention these things to show what can
be done by neat, accurate kicking, and what
should be practised. On the other hand, young
players should remember that they must not

attempt tricks to the detriment of more solid play;
and that it is the first duty of a player, before

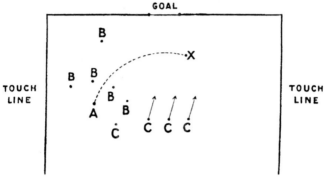

A, player running with the ball. B, B, B, opponents waiting to
tackle him ; they block his path, and he is afraid to pass the ball
lest it should be intercepted. C, C, C, forwards backing up A,
but keeping just behind him, and therefore "on side." x, place to
which A kicks over the heads of B, B. ——➤, lines in which
C, C, C run on A kicking, and thus secure the ball at x before
any of the B players.

anything else is attempted, to learn to kick
accurately into touch.

SAVING.

Now as to "saving," or, in other words, stopping
forward rushes when the ball is being dribbled
along the ground. Far the most effective plan to

stop forwards when they are close upon you is
to fall on the ball; but it must be done in the
right way. A player must not kneel over the
ball, and present his head to the forwards' feet,
for that is most dangerous. He should lie on the
ball, with the ball under his arm-pit, his head
turned away from the forwards, and his back
presented to receive what knocks may come; or,
to put it in another way, he should really be
on the same side of the ball as that on which
the advancing forwards are, and the ball should
be jammed in his arm-pit. In this way there is
little danger of accident, and, usually speaking,
it is not a difficult feat. For instance, when the
ball is kicked just past him, it is quite easy
for him to turn round, throw himself down full
length, and gather the ball under his arm. As
a matter of fact, this is the only thing for him
to do when the ball has been kicked behind him,
for he will have no time to stoop down and pick
it up. But when the ball is in front of him, it
is quite another matter. Then he should certainly
pick up the ball when he can, though, if necessary, he must not have the slightest hesitation
about falling on it. The difficulty under these

circumstances is to decide whether to rush in and pick up the ball, or whether to fall upon it in the manner I have described. Of course, from the spectacular point of view, it seems the smarter play to make a dash and gather the ball; but at the same time there is no good his making a dash if the forwards can kick the ball before he gets to it. No coaching can show to a player when is the right moment for him to dash in ;—it only comes by experience. Yet, perhaps, the best advice to give is this—dash in and try to pick the ball up if there is but half a chance, for in this case boldness is better than caution.

Of all points of three-quarter play, saving from forwards demands the most pluck, the greatest quickness, and the soundest judgment. A smart three-quarter, who knows exactly the right moment to make a dash for the ball, can nip it from under the very feet of the forwards, and perhaps get away himself. Yet few players can do this really well, while I am afraid there are only too many who bungle dreadfully.

A wing three-quarter should always be on the look-out for dashing down on dribbling forwards from the side. Above I have been speaking of a player who is standing right in the path of a forward rush, but a player who is at the side of the line the forwards are taking is in a capital position to stop them. His duty will be to rush in at right angles to the line they are taking, and gather the ball. If this is done well, he may pick up the ball, fly before their very faces, and yet get off. If he cannot do this, he may charge in among them and upset them, and though he may not actually stop them, he may so throw them off the run that another back has no difficulty in getting the ball. Consequently a wing three-quarter should always be on the look out for swooping down from the side on to a forward rush.

TACKLING.

And now to say a few words about tackling, which is an all-important feature of three-quarter play. The first thing that all must learn is to tackle low. By that I mean putting down the head, and charging straight at a man's waist, throwing the arms round him at the same time. The force of the charge alone will probably turn the runner over, but if it does not the runner will

come down as soon as the arms grip, especially
if the tackler give a pull at the same time. This
tackle, of course, is well known, and every boy and
young player should learn it. It is quite easy, you
will find, if a runner is running round you, and
he is not much faster or bigger than you are. You
should get close before you attempt it, and then
down with your head and go straight in. Once
you have done it successfully you will do it again,
and very soon learn to be a "dead" tackler. But,
unfortunately, nowadays this particular form of
tackle cannot always be used. It is all right when
a player is attempting to run round you or away
from you, but it is not easy if a player is coming
straight at you, and, just before he reaches you,
turns. If a player runs straight at you, hoping
you will funk or get out of his way, wait for him ;
then, as he gets quite close, open your arms, stoop
down, and throw yourself forward at his waist,
putting your head, *not* in his stomach, but by his
side. The result will be that the runner comes
right down on his back, with you on the top, or
if you have not managed it quite successfully,
or he has swerved to the side, you may yet bring
him down much in the way that you do when

tackling a person running round you. If you have to tackle a really good dodging runner, your only chance is to rush him. By this, I mean that you must not wait for him, but must dash straight at him, and attempt to tackle him in a similar manner to that which you would employ when trying to stop the ordinary runner. If he is really good you may very possibly miss him ; but it is your best chance.

Moreover, as the game is played nowadays you have to be very careful not to tackle the wrong man. A runner will come up to you, and try to entice you to tackle him ; as you make your rush he passes the ball, and the two of you are left on the ground, while another opponent is off down the field. But this will be more obvious when we have discussed passing and offensive tactics generally.

The Attack.

For the attack there is one golden rule, and that is, when the ball is in your hands run as hard as you can, and as straight as you can, but the moment you find yourself blocked in front pass the ball at once. Remember this, you young three-quarters, and as soon as you see one of your

PASSING THE BALL.

own side in a better position than you are yourself, pass the ball to him. Now, this rule seems
very simple, and it is strange to find how badly
it is often bungled. To begin with, accurate
fielding and accurate throwing are necessary. A
player must be able to give and take a pass
while he is running full speed, and there must be
no stumbling or hesitation. A pass should be
low, that is, it should come to the waist of the
player to whom it is thrown. It should go straight,
not in a curve, and should be thrown rather in
front of the runner, though how much in front
depends of course upon the pace at which the
man who is to receive the pass is travelling. All
this can be learnt from practice on the field, and
should so be learnt and practised diligently; for
passing will never be carried out successfully in a
match until it can be done successfully in practice.

But to resume. Having assumed that a certain
accuracy in giving and taking passes has been
attained, let us see how the three-quarters ought
to stand on the field, and what their duty is
to each other. Let us suppose, in the first instance, that the scrummage is formed close to
the right touch-line. The right wing three-quarter

ought to stand about three or four yards away from the nearest half-back; he should be well behind the half-back, that is to say, quite a couple of yards nearer his own goal; he should also be nearer the centre of the field. The right centre three-quarter should occupy, with regard to the right wing three-quarter, a relatively similar position to that which the right wing three-quarter occupies with regard to the half-back. He should be well behind him, and rather further towards the centre of the field. The left centre and the left wing should occupy similar positions, so that the three-quarter line is stretched right across the field, one behind the other.

The diagram on p. 113 may help to make my meaning clear.

Now, as soon as the ball comes out of the scrummage into the hands of one of the halves, the whole line should commence to run straight forward; the first half will probably pass straight to the second half, and the second half almost at once to the right wing three-quarter. He by that time will have got well under weigh, and if he sees an opening he should dash straight through. If, however, as is more probable, he does not, he should at once pass to the right centre. The latter may now see an opportunity of going straight through, which he should take if he can. If not, he must use his own judgment as to whether he should at once pass to the inside left, which is commendable, or whether he should run a bit and

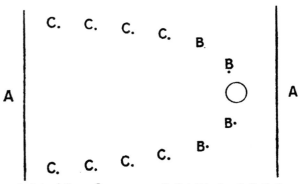

A, A, touch-lines ; O, scrummage ; B, B, half-backs ; C, C, C, C, three-quarter backs.

then pass, or whether he should kick. Supposing he passes to the left-centre, if the passes have all been smart, so that no time has been wasted, the left-centre should have a good chance of getting away. When he receives the ball he should be running nearly at top speed, and he will probably find himself well clear of his opponents. If he has a chance he should run on ; if not, he should pass out to his wing, who will very likely have a still better opportunity of running straight on.

Now, if a three-quarter should break through or slip past the opposing three-quarters, he will find himself with a field more or less clear of his opponents. The full back may be in his way, or able to get in his way ; there is, of course, the further danger of his being cut off by some one running across from the other side of the ground. If, however, he is fairly fast, and has a good lead, there is not much chance of his being tackled in this way. The real problem is how to get past the full back without slackening his speed to such an extent as to give his pursuers, who are hard on his track, a chance of getting up to him. Well, a three-quarter should, in the first place, go straight ahead as hard as he can, and on no account slacken his pace. He then should at once look out for some one to whom he may pass. If he be the wing three-quarter, he should easily find some one inside to whom he may pass. But it is very often the case that a three-quarter gets clean away, and none of his side back him up to

take his pass ; so be it remembered that it is the
duty, particularly of the three-quarters, to back
up any one of their side, and so be in a position
to take the pass. If, however, he finds himself
unsupported, he must make up his mind to try
and dodge the back, or run round him, or, as I
have suggested, punt over his head.

For purposes of illustration, I took an instance
where the scrummage was situated at the side of
the field. But the system is the same wherever
the scrummage may be. Thus, if the scrummage
takes place in the centre of the field, there will
be two three-quarters on either side of it. If half
way between the centre and touch-line, there will
be one three-quarter on the side towards touch,
and three on the other side. In this way there
will always be a little shifting going on amongst
the three-quarters, and it must be left to the
players' own judgment to decide when and how
they shall change their positions.

The Defence.

But so far we have been assuming that the ball
is amongst our own forwards in the scrummage,

and is likely to be passed out by our own halves. Under these circumstances the formation I have explained is the right one. But when the reverse is likely to happen, that is to say, when we see that the ball will probably come out to our opponents, our three-quarters—the two or three nearest the scrummage, at any rate—must draw up; by that I mean they should stand as near the attacking three-quarters as they can without violating the rules. As soon as the ball comes out to their opponents, they should rush straight at the man to whom it will be passed, and try to reach him as soon as the ball does, or even sooner. That, of course, is the simple plan to stop machine-like passing, but in practice it will never quite work out smoothly. There is always a great deal of scope left for the individual genius of each player, which will impel him to dart at this man instead of that, to dodge instead of pass, to kick instead of run. I am thankful that it is so, for this is the peculiar fascination of the game, in that it does call forth and reward individual effort, and that play which can only be termed machine-like is more often beaten than not. In defence, then, a player must use his judgment.

He will soon understand what the other side intend to do, or will try to do, and he must anticipate their plans as far as he can. If he sees two players, one carrying the ball, coming straight at him, he knows that one will come close up, and try to draw his tackle ; that then, just before he tackles him, the man carrying the ball will pass it to his companion ; that his duty is to so contrive as to make one of them give this pass, and then to tackle the other before he passes it in turn. But above all things, he must remember not to let the one who is originally carrying the ball slip away without passing. He must bring him down if there is any chance of that, and must not edge away from him as the runner approaches without making up his mind. As soon as the runner notices his hesitation, he will go straight on, and a player will need to be very sharp to catch him.

QUALITIES NECESSARY.

Before I close these somewhat desultory remarks on three-quarter-back play, I should like to say something about the qualifications for

that position. Speed is what is usually supposed
to be the great desideratum, and by that is
usually meant speed on the racing-path. It is,
undoubtedly, very desirable that three-quarters
should have speed, but speed on a racing-path is
a very different thing to quickness on a football
field. At football you want a player to go thirty
yards, perhaps even fifty, very quickly, and often
a person who goes thirty or forty yards very fast
will only do a slow hundred. Thus it is a great
mistake to think a man is a born three-quarter
if he can run a hundred yards well under eleven
seconds. In a three-quarter you want quickness
and alertness, but above all, "head." In other
words, you want a player of decision, who never
hesitates, but acts promptly, and who also can
anticipate what another player, either on his own
or the opposing side, is going to do. In addition,
a certain amount of sturdiness is absolutely necessary, for without bone and muscle it is rare to
find a player who is sound in his defensive
tactics.

CHAPTER VII.

FULL BACK PLAY.

By Gregor MacGregor,

Scotch International in all Matches, 1890, 1891, 1893, 1894.

I REMEMBER once overhearing a definition of a full back, which I thought
very much to the point. Two
schoolboys were watching a Rugby
game, and presently the younger
of the two inquired, pointing to
the player in question, "What do
they call that man standing over there?" "Oh,
don't you know?" came the answer; "that's the
full back." "But why is he called full back?"
continued his inquisitive companion. There was
a pause—the question evidently presented a difficulty. At last the elder replied, "I don't exactly
know, but Uncle Bill says that he was given the

name because he was the fool on whose back all
the other players laid their mistakes." I cannot
say that in my heart I disagreed from the opinion
so forcibly expressed by Uncle Bill!

Any player who wishes to become a really first-
rate full back should begin at an early age to
practise two of his most important duties, namely,
kicking and fielding the ball. He should learn to
tackle, and must be by nature fearless in "saving"
the ball under the feet of rushing forwards. Experience will in time teach him where to stand as
the game swings backward and forward, and from
side to side of the field. Lastly, there are certain
general details on which I may be able to give him
a few useful hints.

FIELDING.

The quality of a full back is often judged nowadays by his ability to field the ball accurately on
every occasion. Fielding has become exceedingly
important, owing to the "kick-and-rush" style
adopted by so many teams ; especially is this the
case in the North of England, where the wet state
of the ball, consequent on the muddy grounds,
renders fielding most difficult. In the "kick-and-

rush " style of play, the brunt of the work falls on
the full back. He has to face two different
methods of attack. Sometimes the dribbling
forwards, instead of keeping the ball at their feet,
kick it in front of them as hard as they can, and
rushing after it, endeavour to tackle the full back
before he can get in his kick. Woe betide him if
he fumbles with the ball, as they come charging
down upon him ! Sometimes, again, one of the
three-quarters will kick the ball high into the air,
while the forwards race up under it with the same
purpose as before. When they are " off-side," as
is not unusually the case, they crowd up as near
to the full back, who is waiting to catch the ball,
as they think the referee will allow them, instead
of giving him his full five yards clear space. Unless the referee supports him, the full back is,
under such circumstances, in a most unpleasant
position. He may, very probably, if at all a
nervous player, lose his head, and fail to gather
the ball when it falls, in which case the forwards
are at once put "on side," and rush upon him ;
should he, on the other hand, make a fair catch,
they are so close to him that he has not room to
kick. While the full back is expostulating and

demanding his legitimate "five yards," the three-quarter who kicked the ball, or a player behind him at the time, may run up and put the forwards "on side." It is difficult to determine what rule to formulate when a weak referee is controlling the play, but I should strongly advise the full back to make his mark the moment he sees there is a danger of such untoward events occurring.

The full back should never, if he can possibly avoid it, allow the ball to bounce. He should endeavour to catch it as it is falling, for, owing to the formation of the Rugby ball, it is impossible to say with any certainty, when once it touches the ground, in what direction it will twist. I once had a very sad experience at Bradford, which has impressed itself on my memory. It occurred in one of the first matches in which I ever figured as a full back. The London Scottish was the team in which I was included, and I was standing in my own "twenty-five" when the ball was kicked to me. I waited, foolishly, to catch it on the first bounce ; but the ball, with that maliciousness peculiar to Rugby footballs, instead of coming straight to me, shot off at an entirely opposite angle. I must admit that I believe the ball to have been far more pointed than is usually the case. After it I ran, and just as I thought I had gathered it, it bounced again, and back it went to the place I had just come from. How long I should have pursued this refractory piece of leather it is impossible to say, but the hunt was rudely disturbed by a Bradford forward, into whose arms it sprung, rushing off and gaining a try without my ever having touched it at all. I hope this story will be a warning to youthful players, who are liable to put their trust in the philanthropic nature of a Rugby football. I should advise any one who thinks himself fitted to fill the position to commence to learn this part of his work as early as possible. Let him choose some friend while at school, and let the pair of them practise by kicking the ball backwards and forwards from one to the other. It will teach them catching, fielding, and kicking as well.

KICKING.

A full back must be able to punt and drop-kick with either foot. When playing against the wind he should always endeavour to make the ball

land in touch. When playing with a strong wind
behind him, a back may sometimes find it advisable to kick the ball high into the air, in the
hope that the wind will carry it far down the field,
and that the opposing players, when they get hold
of it, will not be able to return it to the place from
whence it came. Punting is far safer than drop-
kicking. In the early days of the game punting
was looked upon with disfavour, though the reason
for its unpopularity is hard to discover. Its value
has now long been recognized ; in fact, it is the
only safe form of kick available for a back when
he is penned by the advancing forwards of the
other side. Another method of kicking is sometimes termed "fly kicking," or taking a kick at
the ball as it is rolling on the ground. This is
a style of play which cannot be too strongly dis-
couraged in a full back. Let him always remember
that he composes the last line of the defence, and
that the play of a man on whom so much
depends should always be on the side of safety.
A sure game brings more credit to a player
than one which consists of occasional brilliant
sparkles.

SAVING.

This is probably the most dangerous part of the game. It requires a man of great pluck and resolution to fall on the ball under the feet of dribbling forwards. A certain number of hacks he must inevitably expect, bestowed, not intentionally, but in their efforts to get the ball away from him. I have always considered that the development of this feature of the game was a great mistake. It spoils dribbling, and seems to put a premium on rough play. Forwards who think of other things besides winning the game, often refrain from hacking when it might be just possible for them to get the ball away by so doing ; on the other hand, players who have lost their temper, or are disappointed in being robbed of the fruits of a long dribble, may not be so scrupulous, and a bad accident may be the result. However, it is part of the game, and is greatly admired by those members of the old school, who still have a sneaking affection for the hacking system. There is no doubt that an alternative means of defence would be most difficult to find, and until found the full back must continue to shield the ball with his body.

Perhaps the most fearless back that ever distinguished himself in this department was J. P. Veitch, of the Edinburgh Royal High School and Scotland. He was absolutely without fear, and would dive at the ball and secure it from under the feet of the roughest forwards that ever played. He seemed absolutely impervious to the kicks which he must constantly have received.

TACKLING.

Tackling is as important as fielding and catching in the play of a full back. Many a time has a good tackler saved his side when an otherwise certain try would have been registered against them. A full back should always tackle low. In any doubtful case he should go for the man with the ball. This is a most important point, and cannot be too strongly insisted on. Often the modern full back has to face two or three men who have got clear of his three-quarters, and come speeding down towards him. He knows that the man with the ball will in all probability run up to him, and then pass it to one of his companions. Yet, unless he actually sees the ball leave that

A HARD TACKLE

player's hands, he should tackle the runner as
hard as he is able. Of course that man may pass
just as the full back tackles him ; but, on the other
hand, he may have delayed too long, and the full
back may secure both the man and the ball. Or,
again, the rush of the full back going strongly at
him, may cause him to make some mistake when
passing, and either throw the ball forward, or
make so bad a pass that the opportunity of scoring
is lost. Nothing appears more absurd to players
and spectators than the performance of the un-
decided full back, who cannot make up his mind
which of the runners to tackle, and having feinted
first at one, and then at another, is finally fooled
by them all—a just punishment for his indecision.

Probably the two finest tacklers that ever filled
the place of full back are H. B. Tristram, the
Oxford International, and R. B. Walkington, of
Ireland. These two men have made reputations
that will long be remembered in the football world.
I should say that the most brilliant piece of
tackling ever done by a full back was accom-
plished by Tristram in a match played between
England and Scotland at Manchester, in 1887.
The English team had not been expected to win,

but "time" was rapidly approaching, and they had scored a try to nothing against their opponents. Five minutes only were left when W. E. Maclagan, who throughout the game had been playing magnificently, got possession of the ball. The Scotchman was, I think I may safely say, the strongest man amongst the two teams, as he was also the heaviest, scaling at this time fourteen stone seven pounds. He slipped by Rotherham, and meeting Lockwood, knocked over the little Yorkshireman as if he had been a fly. He then found himself but five yards from the goal-line, and although his opponents hemmed him in on one side, while the touch-line was but a few feet from him on the other, there was nobody in front of him—save Tristram. He had no room to dodge, even if he had felt inclined to do so, and, putting on his full pace, he charged down upon the Englishman. Tristram did not wait the shock, but sprang to meet him, and the most dangerous scorer near the line that Scotland has ever produced met the finest of English backs with a crash that literally was heard all over the field. Down went the pair of them, and the forwards swept round the prostrate figures; then the spectators saw Tristram emerge, and cheered themselves hoarse in admiration for a piece of play which will never be forgotten by those who witnessed it.

WHERE TO STAND.

A full back can only learn by experience where to stand, as the game changes its position. His judgment in this respect will probably make all the difference between his turning into a good player, or his remaining only a moderate one. When he sees that his own back division are hard at work tackling their opponents, who are advancing, passing from one to the other the while, he should come up close behind his three-quarter line, so as to be able to immediately tackle any opponent who breaks through it. Sometimes the full back will see that the man with the ball is hemmed in, but has a companion running by his side, to whom he will be compelled to pass. Under these circumstances he should mark the second man, and rush at him the moment he receives the ball from the first man, who naturally passes just before he is tackled. If the full back pursues these tactics, he will be able to stop the

I

runners before they have got clean away from his
three-quarters, and have only himself to think about.

If a scrummage takes place nearer one touch-
line than the other, the back should hug that
touch-line, for if the ball is kicked by one of his

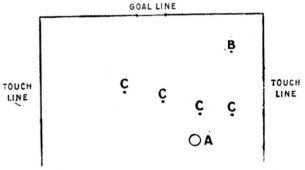

A, the scrummage ; B, the full back ; C, C, C, C, the three-quarters.

opponents, it will in nine cases out of ten be
directed towards the nearest touch-line. He will
have plenty of time to get across the field should
a passing run be started by the opposing three-
quarters. I give above a diagram of his position.
Yet, as I have said before, his own judgment,
born of experience, can alone tell him where to

stand to receive a ball that is kicked over his
three-quarters' heads, or when to tackle a runner
on the best terms.

WHAT TO WEAR.

I should advise every full back to have two
pairs of boots ready ; of these one should be
heavy, and one light. If the ground is muddy,
the ball will become heavy, and plenty of driving
power will be required for long kicking. Light
boots may be worn on dry grounds, for the ball will
be easier to kick and the game faster. I always
found chamois leather the best material for gloves.
It does not become greasy so quickly as do the
harder sorts of leather, and it gives readily to the
hand. I strongly advise a back never to wear a
"sweater," for by it he may easily be tackled.
He should, however, put on a couple of jerseys in
cold weather, for, on a winning side, full back has
often rather a chilly time of it.

GENERAL REMARKS.

Good full backs are undoubtedly scarce. The
reason for this is not far to seek. Few people
care to play full back if they can obtain any other
position in the team. Although a full back enters

into the game in a far less proportion than the other players, he yet has the doubtful satisfaction of filling the most responsible position on the field. A good full back has tackling and kicking powers, which usually make him a fair three-quarter, and, as is perhaps only natural, he is always trying to obtain a place there, or in some other part of the team.

Of players of to-day, the best, in my opinion, is A. R. Smith, of Oxford and Scotland, who combines as nearly as possible all the qualities necessary for the position. He is a fine field, and a splendid kick, being able to drop the ball to within a yard or two of the direction he wishes it to take. Besides being a dangerous tackler at close quarters, he is very fast, and is thus able to pick up an ordinary runner who has slipped past him. W. J. Bancroft, of Swansea, is also a fine player, and has achieved a great reputation for his success in placing and dropping goals from long distances and at difficult angles. In fact, he is probably equal to Smith in every point save tackling. The writer has not, however, seen so much of his play as of the Scotchman's, and is therefore hardly qualified to compare the two closely.

CHAPTER VIII.

THE REFEREE.

I.—HIS HISTORY.

T is not too much to say that the most important man at a modern Rugby football match is the referee. Upon his firmness and decision, his activity and quickness of eye, the whole game depends. Given a man not fitted for the post, you will find grumbling and dissatisfied players, and too often, I am sorry to say, hooting spectators. At the same time, there is no doubt that the behaviour of both players and spectators has improved and is improving. Even amongst the roughest crowds the honesty of the referee is rarely impugned, however much they may cavil at

what they consider the appalling nature of his
mistakes.   There is an old American story, that a
traveller observed a notice hung over the heads of
the two violins and an accordion which composed
the band at a Western dance.   He strolled up to
it, and discovered that it read, " Do not shoot at
the band ; they are doing their best."   That is
exactly the attitude assumed by North-country
football crowds towards referees.   They are now
tolerated, and for that they are thankful, not being
a grasping race, and anxious only for the smaller
mercies.

Through the seventies the feeling had been
growing that the method hitherto adopted of
settling disputes arising in the course of the
games was becoming less and less adapted to the
needs of the situation.   There are plenty of
players of the younger football generation who
will find it difficult to believe that a time ever
existed in the history of Rugby Football when the
captains of the respective sides had sole control
over the game.   Like the inhabitants of the Scilly
Islands, who " earn a precarious livelihood by
taking in each other's washing," the captains
did each other's refereeing, though whether they

comes from practical experience. The player of
an "elder day" must remember that each year
there are changes in the rules, and that it is absurd
for him to stroll on to a football field with the
general idea that he can get on all right by the aid
of his previous knowledge of the game and the
light of nature. In nearly all cases it is just as
well for the referee to carry the book of rules
about with him. Not that he has time to examine
them on an appeal being made; but he may
refresh his memory during a pause in the play, or
even point out a particular ruling to a discontented
player.

In his decisions he must be absolutely firm.
Right or wrong, he must never hesitate. Should
he make a mistake, "tell a lie, and stick to it,"
is the only policy possible. A curious incident
occurred in a match between Cardiff and Swansea
n 1892. A goal was disputed. The referee
himself was uncertain, but said he thought it was
a goal. Subsequently he said he thought it was
not—giving the defending side the benefit of the
doubt. The Welsh committee, before which the
case was brought, decided that, as the decision of
the referee was "irrevocable," his first answer of " I

think it is a goal" settled the matter. The Committee of the Rugby Union have also directed that "a referee having given a decision after blowing his whistle, cannot under any circumstances alter it." The necessity of this is obvious to any player.

A nervous referee was often much troubled by violent appeals. Under such circumstances it was very difficult for him to keep his head. Dr. Almond, the head-master of Loretto school, formulated an excellent rule. "When in doubt," he said, "decide against the side that makes the most noise." At the present time, however, the system of appealing has almost entirely disappeared. The Rugby Union in September, 1893, decided that the referee could, by arrangement, control the game without appeal. He was given the power to blow his whistle whenever he saw a rule broken ; but at the same time he was told not to stop the game when an infringement of the laws by one side was calculated, in his opinion, to benefit the other. In that case no appeal would probably have been made.

A referee must remember that he is expected to work hard, and must dress himself suitably. With the great extension of passing and a faster line when the ball goes into it on their side, and *vice versâ*. This has the advantage of simplicity ; but it is rather a lazy method. The perfect referee will always change his side of the scrummage as play swings from right to left, or left to right, so as to be as near the centre of the field as possible.

Above all things, let the referee procure a good loud whistle. A squeaky little instrument that cannot be heard, and allows players to continue running and tackling each other after it has been sounded, only annoys everybody interested in the game.

To touch judges, selected by their respective sides, I should make one mild suggestion. Pray cheat as little as possible !

CHAPTER IX.

HOW TO CAPTAIN A CLUB.

APTAINS, like poets, are born, and not made. There are some people who imagine that it is quite easy to captain a football team. Let them try and see. Every season the Rugby game becomes more scientific. It has long ceased to be a hurly-burly rout, in which brute strength and good luck were of the first importance. A first-class team is a complex machine, and, like a smart engineer, a captain must watch the various parts of it and see that they are working properly together. There are some ideal captains, whose mere presence in the field encourages the players. They know that their leader will make use of every advantage that fortune or superior skill may send them. Amongst

the game, and seen him subsequently despatch
one or two pairs post haste to the nearest boot-
maker. *À propos* of this, an amusing incident
occurred previous to the England *v.* Scotland
match which was played at Glasgow in 1873.
The ground was greasy, and the English players
adjourned to a local cobbler to have fresh bars
fixed on their boots. After the work had been
done, it was discovered that two boots were miss-
ing. One belonged to Freeman, and another to
Boyle, both Internationals of great reputation.
The shop was ransacked, but the wily cobbler
had hidden them so effectively that they were
not discovered until the next day. There was no
time to procure other football boots, and the two
Internationals had to get along as best they could
under the circumstances. Boyle, I believe, played
with a dress boot on one foot, and his remaining
football boot on the other.

Bars are undoubtedly better than studs of leather.
A stud soon wears away, and not uncommonly
leaves the long nail that fixed it projecting like
the spike of a running-shoe, to the great danger of
friends and foes alike. In the matter of jerseys,
a close-fitting garment of some strong material,

made after the fashion of a vest, with two buttons
in front, is the most workman-like and durable
thing to wear. Rough woollen jerseys, that were
at one time universal, have almost disappeared.
They were very uncomfortable, difficult to put on
or take off, and dangerous for the dye they contained. Of course the vest-jerseys are variously
coloured, and a captain should see that the firm
that supplies the club does not, for the sake of
economy, use cheap and poisonous dyes, which
may work through a cut and cause blood-poisoning. The same remark applies to coloured woollen
stockings.

There is another small point to which I
should like to draw the captain's attention. Do
not have a fresh ball for every match. The larger
clubs have realized that a ball that has been
frequently used is, if well cared for, far superior
for passing, kicking, and dribbling than a new
one. Ground men, possibly with the idea of a
percentage or for the sake of appearances, will try
to produce a new ball on every occasion. Don't
let them do it.

An Englishman's idea of hospitality is limited,
so it is often said, to the consumption of food. It

may be for this reason that football dinners have
increased in number of late years. When a team
goes on tour, it is dined every night by the various
clubs it encounters. When the latter, in their
turn, go touring about the country, it returns the
compliment. They are very pleasant functions,
and increase the "gaiety of nations" to a remarkable extent. I do not at all object to the
mingling of all classes now and again, although
a member of the M.C.C. would be rather surprised
if he were set down to dine between a couple of
obscure professionals. An amusing story is told
of a certain International football dinner, at which
a prominent member of Dublin University found
himself next to a worthy man, who took, indeed,
the greatest care of him, but who had rather a
poor idea of his experience in the art of dining.
"Now you stick to me," he said ; "I'll see you
through. You have not been at one of these
dinners before, and so of course you don't understand all our little arrangements. I see that
card bothers you ; but don't you mind. *Selle
de mouton*, it says. That just means a saddle of
mutton—nothing else, I can assure you. *Homard
aux caramels*" ("ham-boned ox caramels," he

called it) "is only pressed beef and turnips. Now, don't you trouble yourself and get nervous ; I'll tell you all about it as we go along." It is needless to add that they fraternized exceedingly.

While on the subject of dinners, I should like to point out to a captain that large and expensive feasts are absurd. It is merely gratifying the desire for display. Firstly, it burdens young clubs with needless expenses ; secondly, it is bad for training. Plain food is all that is necessary ; and plain food will be fully appreciated by visiting teams who have come on tour to play football, and not, as it would seem is sometimes the case to get the benefit of a cheap excursion. Hunger is said to be the best sauce ; and the hunger that comes from good condition and a hard game is better than all the condiments ever invented by the most skilful of *chefs*, or even the late Mr. Sala himself. Of training, both in the matter of the exercise to be taken and of the food to be eaten, I will speak in another chapter.

SELECTING THE PLAYERS.

It is by no means an easy matter to choose a team when the competitors for the vacant places are numerous, and it is difficult to give any advice worthy of the name as to a theory of selection. Let the captain or committee remember that a man with sound judgment and presence of mind is required for the position of full back, besides skill in tackling and kicking. For wing three-quarter mere pace is not sufficient. Because a man has made a name on the running track, it does not prove that he will be a first-class wing three-quarter. For centre three-quarter, sure tackling, good kicking, and, above all, plucky "saving" are the qualities required. One half, at least, should be a man of strength and weight, to bear the brunt of a losing game behind beaten forwards. As regards the front rank, weight is something, but not everything. Thirteen stone is an ideal weight. "Wingers" who play at the side or back of the scrum should be treated with suspicion. Some teams play one or two wing forwards, who make themselves generally useful by breaking away with a dribble, or hampering the opposing halves and three-quarters. But a captain should see that their example of slacking in the scrummage is not followed by the other forwards. If the front rank all become satisfied in their own minds that they

are the equals of Sam Woods or Evershed, and
insist on attempting to copy their game, disaster
will inevitably follow. To be beaten forward in
nine cases out of ten means to lose the match, for
the backs will never get chances to display their
prowess, however brilliant they may be. A good
goal kick should always be included in the team.
It is extraordinary how little goal-kicking is
nowadays practised, although victory or defeat
may time after time depend upon the efforts of the
man to whom the duty is entrusted. I do not, of
course, recommend a captain to follow the example
of a celebrated Irish committee, who chose an
inferior player "because he could place goals,"
when there was not the slightest chance of their
securing a try from which he might display his
skill.

As a second point it may be asked, "Who is
to do the choosing of the team?" In the big
matches of the year—the International, North and
South, and Inter-County — committees must of
necessity have the power of selection. In these
cases a committee becomes, so to speak, a football
parliament. Many members represent enthusiastic
constituencies, and the fact that grave dissensions

rarely occur, speaks highly for the sportsmanlike qualities of English football players. But in clubs I believe that, as a general rule, the captain should be unfettered in his choice of the team. To this one exception may be made. In schools there is great danger that a captain, when left entirely to his own devices, may show favouritism. The mere suspicion that the captain is acting unfairly is fatal. In the school republic absolute honesty and fair play are the first essentials of success. A boy will never forget his unjust expulsion from a fifteen in favour of some inferior player. He will nurse the grievance, and air it upon every possible occasion. Grumbling is most contagious. It has always appeared to me that the French nation are never so happy as when they are shouting "treachery," and suggesting that some one else is, all things considered, decidedly perfidious. In the same way the average schoolboy is always on the watch for evidences of favouritism. Great care should be taken that he has no reason given him for raising that cry, which he certainly will do if it be in any way possible.

Although, as I have stated above, I am in favour of absolute monarchy, at the Universities

L

and in a large number of well-known clubs a contrary practice prevails. The players are selected by a committee, and under certain circumstances the system works very well. The committeemen must not be cranks, nor so absurdly enthusiastic, as to refuse to listen to their opponents' arguments. In all hotly debated questions on the respective merits of players, the captain should be ultimately referred to for the final decision. Otherwise disaster may follow, for, as Lord Macaulay remarked, it is impossible for an army to be successfully lead by a debating society. Members of a committee have not the responsible feeling of a captain. They can indulge in their partiality for particular players, and for debate at the same time. A captain, again, is deprived of half his authority when offenders know that their inclusion in the team does not depend on their obedience to his orders on the field of play. Last, and by no means least, the captain has opportunities, never afforded to the committee, of judging the real value of a player. To know how a forward shoves you must shove beside him ; to know how a half passes you must take the passes ; to know if a three-quarter is selfish you must be

close up to him when he is making the run, before
you can call his judgment in question. A committee is often composed of elderly players,
opposed to all "new fangled" notions. A captain
is probably the finest, or one of the finest, expo-
nents of the latest style of play. He can appreciate
the advantages or disadvantages of any improvement long before the committee have recovered
from their surprise at the innovation.

A captain must find opportunities for coaching
his team. He can see that the players once or
twice a week meet and practise dribbling, passing,
and goal or place-kicking. Arthur Budd, in his
celebrated article, which dwelt on the advantages
that would accrue to a team from the extension
of passing and the combination of the players,
pointed out that any team might make for itself
name and fame in the football world, provided
that it started with good material, and constantly
practised on the lines indicated. The success of
Vassall's Oxford team, which is now a matter of
football history, proved the truth of his theories.
Vassall, as a method of training his men, adopted
a series of picked games, which, as he himself
subsequently stated, were " far more useful to the

team than the minor foreign matches." With this
view I do not agree. From experience in " picked
fifteens," both in University and county football,
I have come to the conclusion that the worst
possible football is exhibited by those who take
part in them. Each player plays for himself
alone. He knows that the eyes of the committee
are bent upon him, and reserves himself for opportunities of smart play where smart play can be
seen and admired by them. The game is invariably
rough, and the tempers of all concerned disappear
in a few minutes. It is far better for a committee
of a county to visit the leading inter-club matches ;
for a University captain or committee to watch the
inter-college matches, where the greatest keenness
prevails ; for a club captain or committee to super-
intend the matches of their second or third fifteens.
It is in games such as these where the honour of the
club is at stake, and players are not merely actuated
by the desire for personal glorification, that the true
form of a man or boy may be observed and noted.

ON THE FOOTBALL FIELD.

Let us now consider the position of the captain
when the match is fixed, the team chosen, and

amid the applause of his supporters, he leads his men on to the field of play. Here he is absolute —there can be no doubt about that. There is no committee to suggest trivialities to him. Perhaps the best description of the perfect football captain in the field is that given by the late Judge Hughes in "Tom Brown's Schooldays." "Over all," he wrote, "is old Brooke, absolute as he of Russia, but wisely and bravely ruling over willing and worshipping subjects, a true football king. His face is earnest and careful as he glances a last time over his array, but full of pluck and hope —the sort of look I hope to see in my general when I go out to fight." You were right there, Judge Hughes! There is but little difference between the great general and the great football captain. The same spirit animates them both ; the same qualities give them their victories, or help them to stave off crushing defeats. After all, football is still a "friendlie kinde of fyghte," just as it was in the year 1583, when Puritan Stubbes orated against it.

In the field the football captain is much in the position of the cricket captain. As the latter changes his bowling, and possibly the order of going to the wicket, according to whether the day is wet or fine, and the wicket slow or fast, so the former should change the style of play of his team, according to the vagaries of the weather. There is nothing to be gained by "heeling out" a wet, greasy ball, that neither halves nor three-quarters can make certain of holding. Under these circumstances let the forwards wheel and rush, not picking up the ball, but dribbling all they can. On a fine day let the backs have the ball more frequently, and let the forwards occasionally try bouts of short, sharp passes, instead of rushing dribbles.

The captain should take any advantage in wind or slope that the toss may give him. In cricket, to win the toss means to "go in," with few exceptions. In rowing, a crew can generally "hang on" somehow to the finish if they have secured a good lead. In Rugby football the team will, with the wind or the slope, probably secure the first advantage, and is naturally encouraged thereby. It is a point worth remembering. In kicking off, let the captain, if he takes that duty upon himself, attempt high rather than long kicks. I do not mean short kicks just over the nearest forwards' heads, for the players are, nowadays, scattered all over the field to prevent such tricks proving successful, but high,

long kicks, which will give his own forwards time
to rush up as the ball hangs in the air, and to
tackle the opponent who receives it before he
can return it with a drop or punt. Forwards are
apt to get slack in this "following up," and the
captain should keep them up to the mark. An
immense amount of ground is won if this piece of
play is brought off successfully, and I have, on
several occasions, seen it result in a try. At the
same time the captain must keep an eye on the
over-anxious forwards, to see that they do not
start running too soon, and get in front of the
ball and off-side before it is kicked. This means
a scrummage, and all the advantage of the kick-off
is lost.

I mentioned that it was now the practice to
send some forwards back just before the kick-off.
I append a plan (p. 168) showing the best arrangement of the field on such occasions.

It is a difficult matter to decide which is the
place in the field most suitable for a captain to
occupy. If he is a three-quarter he can see that
the passing works smoothly, but then he is unable
to see how the forwards are behaving in the
scrummage, or if he sees they are playing badly, he

cannot get at them to tell them so. If he is a
forward he knows little of the play of the halves
and three-quarters. If the captain is a member of
the back division, I should advise him to appoint
a lieutenant from amongst the forwards who can
watch the play of his companions. Such a man

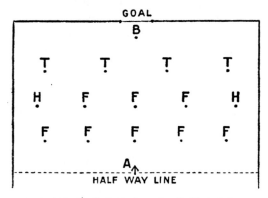

A, the kick-off ; F, F, the forwards ; H, H, the halves ;
T, T, the three-quarters ; B, the full back.

can tell them when to heel out, and which way to
screw. He can see that they are marking their
men at the throw-out from touch, and have fallen
into their right positions at the kick-off. When
a team consists of experienced players, who are

BEFORE THE KICK OFF

certain to keep their wits about them and their eyes on the ball, the less talking that occurs the better. On the other hand, if the team is composed of young and inexperienced players, the lieutenant I have mentioned, or one of the half-backs, should shout instructions as to " heeling " and " screwing," the details of which have been explained in the chapter on forward play. The halves should also shout when the ball is away, that the forwards may break up quickly.

It is fairly obvious that a captain requires a great deal of tact. A few judicious words of praise will effect extraordinary improvement in a young and keen player. He should be firm with evil-doers, but, at the same time, should never growl at his men until they get sulky. He must never make use of stronger language than is absolutely necessary. I cannot thus conscientiously recommend the selection of a captain for the reason given by a member of a rustic fifteen in sunny Devon. " What did you choose him for ? " I queried. " He isn't a bit of good." " Well, zur," answered the rustic, " it's a treat for to 'ear 'im—'e do swear so ! " I have always found that the best coaches in all forms of

athletics temper justice with mercy. A bully
never teaches a man anything except to control
his temper. I well remember a famous Cambridge
rowing coach, with the kindest of hearts and the
most forcible of expressions, who pulled up his
horse, and gazed at the eight he was instructing
more in sorrow than in anger. We sat expecting
to be blasted by his winged words. Nothing of
the kind, however, occurred. " Do you know what
you men are rowing like ? " he asked quietly.
No one answered. " Well, you're rowing as if you
were rowing at a funeral, and were afraid of
bumping the hearse. Paddle on, cox ; " and we
went on our way sorrowing. Those few words
had a far greater effect than if he had used the
most powerful expressions in his well-stocked
vocabulary. Sometimes a captain or coach—
whether he figures on the football field, towing-
path or cricket ground it makes no matter—seems
to each neophyte to take a personal interest in
his individual improvement. Such a man is given
divine honours by the youngsters, and, as a natural
result, they make every effort to please him by
following out his instructions.

A great captain, then, is a man who thoroughly

knows the game, who by example as well as by precept expounds the best method of play, and who has the power of keeping his men in hand. He need not be a great talker. Those who know him will understand what he means without a long explanation. A story which exemplifies this is told of a celebrated Cambridge International, whose motto might well have been *Facta non verba*. He once sent for his college team, of which he was captain, in order that he might give them a few last words of advice before an important match commenced. When they arrived there was a great silence. The team waited open-mouthed for the words of the oracle, and the oracle seemed in difficulties. At last the words came : " When you tackle a man," said he, " don't let him get up in a hurry ; " and the interview closed. They obeyed him to the letter, and won the match hands down.

The chapter has been a long one, but I hope that the hints it contains will be of use to those in authority who are as yet unused to the grave responsibilities which they have taken upon their shoulders in consenting to hold office in a Rugby football club.

CHAPTER X.

HINTS ON TRAINING.

SEVERE training is impossible for a Rugby football player. In running or rowing, athletes go through a careful preparation, but then they have only one particular race or series of races in view. They can thus be trained "to the hour," or, in other words, be ready to run or row on a certain day, though, should that day be suddenly changed to a week earlier, they might not be "in condition," while a week later they might be over-trained and "stale." The football player, who has to play twice a week for four or five months, could not stand the strain of severe training during the whole period. The danger of his becoming "stale" would be too great. At the same time, he must take certain steps to keep

himself fit and well, for the tendency of the game
is to get faster every season, and "the fitter, the
faster," might be called a recognized football
maxim. The backs no longer have time given
them to get their wind while the forwards are
mixed up in a ten-minute scrummage; the
forwards no longer saunter from scrummage to
scrummage, under the idea that to push hard is
the whole duty of man, for they know that they
are expected to be always on the ball, and show
the pace and tackling powers that were considered
the special attributes of the three-quarters. What
a football player requires is to keep in perfect
health during the football season, and in this
chapter I propose to give him a few hints on the
subject that may be of use to him.

For schoolboys no self-denial is necessary, as
far as the school diet is concerned. It is sure to
be simple and wholesome, and that is all that is
required. An energetic school captain should see
that none of his "men" indulge inordinate desires
for jam-puffs or sweetmeats of any description.
The digestion of a growing schoolboy is second
only to that of the ostrich, yet the occasional
tin-tack, which is supposed to be regarded as a

bonne bouche by that eccentric bird, would do him
far less harm than the continual bull's-eye. Of
course, to a great extent, this abstinence from
"grubbing" must be left to the schoolboy honour.
It is impossible to watch each member of the
team in the same manner as did the backers of
pugilists in the old times, when spies were set
to observe if the noted "pets" ever sneaked into
a public-house. That each boy will get regular
exercise, I take for granted. This subject will,
however, be fully dealt with in the chapters on
school football, contained in the present book.

The Universities are somewhat in the same
position as the schools. Of course the University
man has many temptations, radically opposed
to all notions of training, from which the schoolboy is exempt. But he is in the first flush of
manhood, and his recuperative powers are marvel-
lous. He is much in the open air, he takes hard
exercise of some sort every afternoon, and he has
no cares—save his bills and the thought of his
next examination—to worry him. Even the
immediate prospect of the great football event of
the year—the Inter-University match—does not
send him into anything like strict training. He

turns out at eight o'clock, or thereabout, and has a sharp walk ; his captain will sometimes suggest to him that it would be well if he was not *always* seen with a pipe in his mouth. There, however, his training begins and ends in the majority of cases, though there are a few zealous individuals who make an effort to prepare themselves thoroughly. With plenty of fresh air and plenty of hard exercise it is not difficult to keep the muscles hard and the wind good. At the same time, there is little doubt that the play of a University team might be improved by a more regular training. Those who are keen enough to take a little trouble with themselves while at the University, might glance through the following remarks, which, however, I wish particularly to address to the large body of men who have left school and college, and settled in some regular business or profession.

It is naturally difficult for men, especially those who have a tendency to lay on adipose tissue, to sit in their office or chambers for five days in the week, and then play a hard game of football on the afternoon of the sixth. Yet a player, even under these circumstances, can keep fairly fit with

a little care. To begin with, he should make a
habit of early rising ; not the early rising recommended by the intolerable William Cobbett, who
apparently considered that four o'clock in the
morning was the very latest hour at which a
virtuous and well-intentioned young man might
leave his bed, but the early rising which means
being down at a quarter to eight, so that there
may be time for a sharp walk before breakfast
at 8.30.   That morning walk is of great importance.   I do not believe in running hard or
taking any very violent form of exercise.   The
short, quick walk is the best "pipe-opener" on
which to commence the day.   After getting out
of bed and just after the bath, five minutes'
exercise with Indian clubs, dumb-bells, skipping-
rope, or a machine for working the muscles should
always be taken.   In the evening, a walk of some
two miles or so, varied by short sprints at top
speed, is also necessary.   Of course, if a man can
walk or bicycle to his work, let him by all means
do so. If, again, he is skilled in boxing or fencing
let him keep up his practice in these forms of
exercise ; they encourage activity and harden,
without stiffening, the muscles—two important

points in football training. Rowing is, in my
opinion, fatal to football. It stiffens a man, and
materially reduces his pace. Many will probably
disagree with me on this question, but I think I
am correct.

As far as diet is concerned, the plainer the
food the better. This is a hard saying to strong,
healthy men with good appetites, but it is nevertheless true. If a man wishes to diet himself in
a proper manner, he should take fish or a chop,
with fruit to follow, for breakfast ; a light lunch of
some cold meat and lettuce ; and a dinner of fish,
fowl, or the lighter meats, concluding with a sweet
course of stewed fruit or rice-puddings. A man
who has the time, and wishes to actually train
hard, should take regular exercise every afternoon in addition to the work previously suggested.
The best method of preparation both for his wind
and his skill consists in sprinting hard up and
down a field with one or two friends, either
dribbling or passing a ball from one to the other.

Then there is the question of smoking. Few
football players leave their pipes in the rack
during the season, yet tobacco undoubtedly affects
the heart and incidentally the wind. Oarsmen

M

know this only too well, and the first rule in their training is that no tobacco in any form or under any circumstances shall be allowed. Of course rowing a hard race is by far the most exhausting form of exercise, and to it football cannot be for a moment compared. The pipe, then, must remain a matter for the individual conscience.

About drinks between meals there can be no two opinions. I should not wish to impose upon Rugby football players the strict training rule, that only a certain amount of liquid shall be consumed during meals. Let a man satisfy his natural thirst by all means, but—and on this I must insist—let him give up the drinks between meals. If a player, who has to sit on an office stool or in a heated law court, drinks beer, it will cause him to put on fat at a most surprising pace. Spirits are bad for the digestion, and so hit him in another way. Many men take a "night-cap" in the form of a stiff whisky and soda. The word "night-cap" is ludicrously inappropriate, for spirits taken late at night stimulate the heart's action just as that organ should be slowing down for the night's rest, and thus either prevent sleep altogether or keep the sleeper restless and uneasy. Late hours are inevitable to many men, but they should be avoided as far as possible. Lastly, make a point of sleeping with your window open in all weathers, wet or dry, warm or cold. Any hospital assistant will tell you how necessary it is to have plenty of fresh air in a sleeping room.

When a team is on tour, the heavy football dinner which is so often hospitably but injudiciously provided should be avoided as far as politeness admits. Let the men rise early, and take a short walk before breakfast. In the morning, the billiard-room with its stale and stuffy atmosphere should be left severely alone. Moderate sight-seeing may be indulged in ; but the men must remember that few things will tire them more than walking round with their heads in the air. A substantial lunch should be eaten. Nothing is gained, as some players seem to imagine, by appearing on the field of play in a state of semi-starvation. Of course the food must be plain, and no pastry should be included in the bill of fare. Above all things, let them avoid cheese —the most indigestible of eatables. For drink, draught ale is the best. Bottled ale should be avoided, as should any mineral water of a gaseous nature. After the match, they should change as soon as possible. A hot bath is a necessity, but they must not half boil themselves in it, for they thereby incur a great danger of catching subsequent colds. It is perhaps almost unnecessary to say that every member of the team should provide himself with a really warm "sweater" and scarf to wear on the ground before and after the game.

The tendency in modern Rugby football is, as I have already stated, to make the game faster. If professionalism increases to any great extent, —as increase I fear it must — the professional players will, for the sake of the spectators who pay the bills, see that the play gets no slower ; in fact, the rules may tend to approach nearer to those in vogue in the American game. However this may be, it is certain that with faster play more scientific training will become necessary. At present Mr. Whitney, an American whom I have previously quoted, writes, " It would be utterly impossible to fit our football players on the slight training done by the Englishmen, whose season of preparation is very much shorter, and whose game is simplicity itself compared

A DRIBBLE—ALL BY HIMSELF.

to ours." But this is the beauty of our football.
It is at present an amateur game, which can
be played once or twice a week—and played
successfully—without any extraordinary amount
of training. The barrister or member of the
Stock Exchange can be at his work all the week,
and enjoy his game on the Saturday. This is
a point which Mr. Whitney notes and admires :
" It is in the lesser preparation and 'business,' if
I may use the word — and I hope I shall be
correctly interpreted—that lead up to and sur-
round our athletic contests that the Englishmen
set a good example." That is it. We amateurs do
not want to make a " business " of a famous sport.

The Welsh teams have a great reputation for
their magnificent combination and good condition.
A few remarks on what they consider to be sufficient training from the pen of that celebrated
International forward, Mr. C. B. Nicholl, may be
of interest.

" It is a very general mistake," Mr. Nicholl writes
to me, " to suppose that Welsh football players do
an enormous amount of training. This is entirely
wrong. In an ordinary way the members of the
leading clubs train together for about an hour on

one night only in the middle of the week. On
two or three occasions during the season, before
particularly hard matches, an extra night's work
may perhaps be indulged in ; but this is quite
exceptional. It is generally believed in Welsh
football circles that excessive training is not only
unnecessary, but detrimental. All that is required
is that the players look well after themselves in
the everyday habits of life, and take their moderate
amount of exercise regularly and thoroughly.
Every big club has its trainer, bath-rooms, and
gymnasium, and it is there that most of the work
is done. Newport, in particular, has a very fine
building for the men to train in. It is there that
their men take all their exercise, running up and
down at full speed, and passing the ball to each
other. This teaches a man to be in the right place
when waiting for a pass, and allows him to give and
take the ball while travelling at top speed. Then,
to finish up the night's work, they often have a
short game of football under the Association rules.

" Not a small factor in the success of Welsh clubs
is their good fortune in being able to keep the
same, or nearly the same, men together year after
year. Take, for instance, Newport. It is quite

surprising how few changes have been made in this team during the last four years. Indeed, the marked success of this excellent club is in no small degree due to the wonderful combination of both forwards and backs, and to a thorough knowledge of each other's play. Of course, when playing eight forwards against nine, it is obvious that every man must be an honest worker in the 'scrum,' in addition to being quick in the open and good at handling the ball. Thus it is absolutely necessary for the forwards to keep 'fit' during the season. The Welsh game may be at times risky, and doubtless it has a tendency to increase scoring; but I hardly think that any one who has actually played, and had experience of both systems in a first-class team, can doubt that it naturally produces a far more exciting and interesting game than when the three three-quarter system was alone in vogue. The opinions of critics who hold that, under the Welsh method, forwards are reduced to mere heeling-out machines, are worth very little. It will be found that these critics are in almost every instance mere theorists, with very little practical experience in the modern game.

" Naturally the training for International matches is more severe than for ordinary club games. Still, provided the man lives a healthy life, really hard training is quite unnecessary. It can be so easily overdone, and this great danger should be guarded against at all costs. A slightly under-trained man is of very much more value to his side than one who is ' stale.'

" Not a few of the Welsh International players have been produced from Llandovery school. Indeed, this institution has for many years been justly noted for its football. It is a game naturally well suited to the strong, sturdy physique of the Welsh boy, and it is the game which he enjoys and excels in. Here, again, the training is by no means severe ; much the same, in fact, as that at an ordinary English Rugby-playing school. Numerous sides and Form-games are played during the week, and generally a match on the Saturday. Boys are thoroughly drilled in the rudiments of the game when young, and as they grow older they naturally improve in physique and the skill which practice alone teaches."

CHAPTER XI.

A CHAPTER OF ACCIDENTS.

O talk of surgical matters in connection with a popular game seems rather lugubrious; yet I think that a few practical hints may prove useful to players. Although, as has been stated previously, there is a tendency in modern Rugby football to make the game more gentle rather than more violent, accidents will nevertheless occur even in the best regulated football families. Not that the "butcher's bill" is high, when the number of players is considered. According to an article which appeared some years back in the *East Anglian Daily Times*, compiled from statistics supplied by an assurance society, the average is exceedingly low in

comparison with other sports which do not arouse a tenth of the outcry. "Here," says the paper just mentioned, "are the statistics compiled by the assurance company in respect of accidents at various sports. Two months were taken—January and June, 1890—as representative of winter and summer sports respectively. The January claims were: Riding, 40; football, 23; hunting, 19; shooting, 8; dancing, 5; boxing, 4; hockey, 2; bowls, 2 (how in the world did they hurt themselves at bowls?); skating, billiards, dumb-bells, tennis, golf, 1 each—total, 108. The June claims were: Riding, 40; cricket, 34 (compare that with football, ye cricketers who talk about it as a brutal game!); cycling, 31; tennis, 17; rowing, 10; swimming, 6; rinking, 3; polo, 3; shooting, 2; bowls (again!) and wrestling, 1 each—total, 148." From a study of these statistics, I should strongly recommend anxious parents to absolutely forbid their children to play cricket. They should, further, warn them against dancing and bowls, pastimes which, under an innocent and harmless exterior, carry death and destruction amongst those who are attracted by them. The reckless youth who indulge in billiards and dumb-bells should also be instructed in the dangers they incur while following those fascinating pastimes.

Joking apart, I think we may all conclude that football is not such a very dangerous game, after all. The majority of the accidents which occur are, I believe, due to the carelessness of the players themselves. A three-quarter tackles a man very low, yet keeps his head well in front of him, and gets "kneed" on the head by the runner. A half falls on the ball "head on "to the rushing forwards, instead of in the manner suggested in this book by Mr. C. J. N. Fleming. A player—whether forward or back it does not matter—tries to bring off a piece of "gallery" play by jumping over the opposing full back, or diving head first into the midst of the forwards without looking or caring where he is going. It may be that a captain or committee anxious for gate-money insist on playing a game on a frost-bound ground. The Rugby Union have refused to delegate to the referee the power to decide whether the ground is playable or no. I think this was hardly wise on their part, although, as it was argued, the players are the men to suffer if accidents occur, and therefore the right of veto should be in their hands. Last, but not least, the player's football get-up may be to blame. Buckles on belts may leave horrible scratches; rings are dangerous in "handing off" a tackling opponent; worst of all, perhaps, are the nails which are sometimes left exposed in the boots, owing to the leather of the bars they fasten being worn away. A football player with what is practically a running spike in his boot is a dangerous friend or foe.

To take the commonest of the minor accidents —that of a bruise. If it is really bad, an ice-bag should be put on it to reduce the swelling; otherwise, cold water bandages are the best things to apply. Do not bathe the place in warm water, or rub on embrocations at first. Embrocations are excellent things for slight strains or stiffness, but they irritate bruises, and do far more harm than good. If the skin is broken, and there is any chance of dirt getting in, wash the cut at once with water mixed with some antiseptic. Boracic acid, which any chemist will give you, is perhaps the best.

À propos of cuts, players must remember that in wearing cheap woollen jerseys of brilliant hues they run a great risk of blood-poisoning. If dye gets into a wound, it may be a very serious matter. I can myself remember one football team that started to wear jerseys of a peculiar shade of green. The faces of nearly all the forwards broke out into strange eruptions that puzzled the medical men, until at last it was discovered that they were caused by the jerseys. The rough wool rubbed their cheeks and ears in the scrummage, and the poisonous dye gradually worked its way under the skin. It is perhaps needless to say that the jerseys were at once abandoned. Cheap coloured stockings are equally dangerous. A hack breaks the skin, and then the dye works into the wound. The majority of football players will, in all probability, know themselves of such cases, which are not of uncommon occurrence.

Players are often careless in selecting their boots. A well-fitting boot is as important to a football player as to a soldier, and in the service it used to be said that the army won which had the soundest feet. If the boots are too tight, corns are formed very quickly, and, what is still more disabling, bad blisters are raised. If a blister appears, prick it with a needle and squeeze out the water, but be careful to leave the loose, flabby skin to protect the new skin which is forming underneath.   If this loose skin is rubbed off, the sore will take a considerable time to heal.   If the feet seem too tender, a nightly soak in strong salt and water will harden the skin.

A sprained ankle is unfortunately a not uncommon accident.   Though the sprain is but slight, it must not be neglected.   It is not so very long ago that hot water was recommended to reduce the swelling that comes from such a sprain.   This is absolutely incorrect.   Hot water will relieve the pain, but it will have no other effect on the swelling.   When a player sprains his ankle, carry him home, taking great care that he does not use the injured foot.   Then put him on a sofa, and apply an ice-bag to the sprained part.   Cold water and ice is the treatment required.

The knees of football players are, from the nature of the game, peculiarly liable to injury. Many a fine player—like the half-back, Martin Scott—has been cut off almost at the beginning of his career by a damaged knee, which forbade his playing in the future.   The commonest form of accident is a bad sprain, followed by what is known as water on the knee.   The knee becomes puffy and swollen. Under these circumstances, let the injured man lie upon a sofa, keeping the leg level with, or perhaps slightly higher, than his body. Keep an ice-bag on the knee, and bandage it so that he is not able to bend it. If ice cannot be obtained, use lead lotion mixed with spirits of wine. The spirits of wine rapidly evaporate, and thus keep the knee cool. When the water has quite disappeared, and the swelling has been reduced, liniments may be used, and the knee worked to regain its strength. But while any water remains never rub the knee nor apply liniments; the only result of such a proceeding is to increase the inflammation.

Another knee accident is the dislocation of the cartilages of the knee-joint. This is caused by a sudden twist, and may be done by the runner himself without any assistance from a violent tackler. Water will immediately form, and the only thing to be done is to put a long back splint of board or stick down the back of the leg, so that the injured man cannot move the knee-joint, and then carry him home and send for a doctor. The worst feature of this is that once the cartilages have been dislocated, the knee is never quite so strong as it was before, and the accident may occur again at any time. Many players have been compelled to give up football owing to the constant recurrence of this knee trouble. If ever you notice a runner suddenly give a half turn, and then bowl over like a shot rabbit, you will know he has been cursed by that terrible infliction "a football knee."

A player is fortunate if he does not get "winded" once or twice in a season. It is not a serious matter, although the process of coming round is decidedly painful. When a player is "winded," lay him on his back and stretch out his legs, which he will naturally wish to double up. Loosen his jersey about the neck, and undo a button or two of his football shorts. Do not let all the players stand round in a dense, stifling ring, but let him have plenty of air. Then pull his arms above his head, and press them down again to his sides, continuing the process of artificial respiration until he is all right again. As a matter of fact, unless in a very bad case, the artificial respiration is unnecessary.

The accidents of which I have hitherto spoken have been of the simplest kind. I will now mention a few of a more serious nature. In these cases follow out the instructions I give, unless, of course, there is a doctor present who can assume all responsibility ; but the services of a doctor will certainly be required, and the sooner one can be found the better for the injured player.

It is not very difficult to see whether or no a player has broken his collar-bone. The arm is supported by the collar-bone, and if that bone be fractured, the weight of the arm will pull the broken piece down, and create a hole in the bone which can be felt by the finger. Further, the weight of the arm is painful, and the injured man will probably hold his elbow up with his other hand to ease the pain. As a general rule, if you notice a player who has fallen heavily on his shoulder, subsequently supporting his arm in this position, you will know that his collar-bone has "gone." All that can be done is to put the arm in a sling, and then send him off to find a doctor. It is more difficult to tell a broken rib, but if the player seems in pain, give him the benefit of the doubt and pack him off. If a doctor is not at once to be obtained, bandage his side tightly, and keep him as quiet as possible until he arrives.

N

A broken leg can be told by the altered shape. Lay the player on his back and obtain two splints. Narrow boards are the best, for the edges project, and the bandage grip them instead of the leg itself, as is the case when sticks are used. Place the splints one on each side of the broken bone, and tie bandages round them so that the whole leg becomes immovable. The great danger to be avoided is that of a compound fracture where the end of one of the broken bones makes a hole through the skin. A simple fracture may be turned into a compound fracture if carelessly treated. I may add that if no splints are procurable, the two legs may be bound tightly together, the second doing the duty of a splint. Should the thigh-bone be fractured, a long splint is required, reaching from under the arm-pit down to the ankle. In the army a musket is used, the butt resting under the arm-pit. In all these cases the greatest care should be taken in moving the injured man. A hurdle or a door, with men at each corner, will make a fair improvised ambulance ; or, again, two poles with a rug between them on which the man may lie.

A broken arm must be treated in the same

manner as a broken leg. It should be placed in splints, and then bandaged closely to the side. When this is done the player can walk a short distance, if it is necessary for him to do so, without any further injury to himself.

Do not attempt to tamper with a dislocation. Sometimes a man who has a superficial knowledge of the subject will try to do so, but he generally makes matters worse instead of better. Remember that the sooner the bone goes back into its socket the better, for when the dislocation has become cold and stiff it becomes a dreadfully painful affair to reduce it. Send, therefore, for a doctor as fast as you can.

A finger is often broken or dislocated. If a finger is broken there is deformity ; unusual movement may be noticed when it is touched. If it is dislocated there is no deformity, but the finger becomes immovable and stiff. I may allow a finger to be an exception from my rule on dislocations, for it may often be slipped back into its socket with very little trouble. But let a doctor do the necessary work if it be possible.

In cases of concussion of the brain, lay the player on his back with some slight support under

his head. Do not give him brandy. This should
be carefully remembered, for brandy is generally
kept in the pavilion, and administered whenever
an accident occurs as a matter of form. If an
ice-bag can be procured it may be put upon his
head ; but send at once for a doctor, and await his
decision. The rare case of a fractured jaw is occasionally reported. If—though this is extremely
improbable—such an accident happens, tie a broad
soft handkerchief under the chin and round the
top of the head, supporting the jaw.

I do not think there is much more to be said.
I have written as simply as possible, avoiding all
medical terms. If football players will remember
these hints they will at least save the doctor a
great deal of unnecessary trouble, and the injured
man a great deal of unnecessary pain.

One fact that is worthy of notice is, that the
older the football player grows the more wary
he becomes. A novice invariably gets his ears
injured in the scrummage, or gets his wind taken
once in every ten times he is tackled. Not so
the accomplished player. He knows "how to
fall," and that is a great art. A fall to a man
who takes no further exercise than walking from

his house to the railway-station may be a very serious affair; but let that man remember that this is not the case with the football player, who from his youth has been trained to fall lightly and easily under any circumstances.

CHAPTER XII.

A MODERN GAME OF RUGBY FOOTBALL.

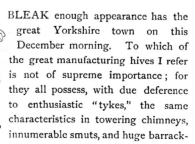 BLEAK enough appearance has the great Yorkshire town on this December morning. To which of the great manufacturing hives I refer is not of supreme importance; for they all possess, with due deference to enthusiastic "tykes," the same characteristics in towering chimneys, innumerable smuts, and huge barrack-like buildings, from which pour the hollow murmurs or loud clangings of machinery. There has been a nip of frost in the night, but not enough to spoil the game—so the telegraph, at least, has told our captain. Twelve o'clock strikes as we emerge from the station and pile our bags on the hotel omnibus. Two of the committee-men of the club we are to encounter have joined us, and are now

walking ahead with our secretary, talking earnestly. From the look of their backs, I should judge that the "gate" is under discussion, and that they are pleased with the financial outlook. After the three we straggle up the street, laughing and talking amongst ourselves.

It is not far to the hotel, and the old campaigners amongst us press on to secure the best rooms. Like the veterans that they are, they have learnt to take matters comfortably between their battles. By the time the young and inexperienced have climbed to the top floor, these gentlemen, having appropriated the rooms lower down, are engaged in finding out the position of the baths, and securing the keys to make doubly sure of obtaining priority in ablutions, and the necessary quantity of hot water ; the kitchen boilers not infrequently give out under the strain put upon them, and nothing is more disagreeable than a cold bath after an hour's roll in the mud. By half-past twelve all these arrangements are concluded, and the majority of us stroll out to inspect the town. Not that there is much to be seen. "It's all rot calling this place a busy hive!" says one of our men to a friend who has ventured upon that metaphor,

"The men may work like bees—I admit that—
but no bees could stand this smoke; they would
have their toes in the air in about three seconds."

However, if there is little to be seen, we have
the satisfaction of knowing that we attract considerable attention. The great Welsh forward
stalks along, a giant in our midst, "the cynosure
of neighbouring eyes." Broad in the back, lean
in the flank, with a small head well set upon his
great shoulders, he looks the tower of strength that
we know him to be. "Gawd, Bill!" we hear one
little boy remark to his companion as we pass,
with that profanity which is the most manly of
qualities in the youthful mind, "suppose 'e was to
fall on yer?" Then there is the braw Scotch laddie
who, so rumour hath it, wore football jerseys in the
nursery, and was playing three-quarter for his
country at an age when most boys are struggling
with the Pons Asinorum. Best known of all, perhaps, are the three thick-set English Internationals
who figure amongst our forwards. Their mighty
deeds are familiar to half the passers-by, and those
who recognize them stop and look back and criti-
cize in whispers. Amongst such a goodly company we, who are as yet unknown to fame, feel that

our feet are upon the bottom rungs of her ladder.
Basking in the radiance that springs from these
heroes, we become more confident, and walk with
a firmer step ; for when the demi-gods are with us,
how can the might of man prevail ?

At 1.15 the team assembles for lunch in the hotel.
Cold beef and beer are provided in no stinted quan-
tities. After the beef is disposed of, cheese is
placed on the table, and two men help themselves
in a hesitating manner. But the captain's eye is
upon them. " Of course you men can eat what you
like," he says severely, " but, in my opinion, to play
football on cheese is—well, is the very deuce." The
argumentative member of the team joins in at
once. " Nothing of the sort," he says ; " it digests
the other food." " But it doesn't digest itself,"
says the captain ; and the men who have taken the
cheese put it ostentatiously at the side of their
plates and call for butter. But the argumentative
man is not to be beaten like this. " My dear fellow,"
he says, " you are a crank on training. Waiter,
bring me the cheese," and he helps himself to a
chunk. The captain makes a short reply, which is
scarcely worthy of minute description. Remember,
you gentlemen who row or run, training is almost

unknown on a Rugby tour, and it is only enthusiastic captains who ever try to interfere with what
the men eat or drink.   At the same time—I speak
from   painful   experience—cheese   " is   the   very
deuce," as our friend the captain tells us, and so
will the argumentative man find out by half-time
this afternoon ; but advice is a waste of words to
a man of his temperament.

At half-past two we retire to our rooms, and in
a few minutes reappear in the workman-like outfit
of an English football player : jerseys—or rather
stout vests,—over which warm woollen sweaters
are drawn ; a " blazer " of the club colours ; a good
thick   scarf   twisted   round   the   neck ;   football
" shorts " of blue serge, without a belt or any such
dangerous contrivance for keeping them in position ; stockings and boots with stout leather bars
across the sole to keep us from slipping.   One or
two of the forwards come down swinging ear-caps
in their hands.   These are contrivances for keeping
the ears close to the head.   It not infrequently
occurs that a player has his ears pulled forward
and injured by the pressure of the scrummage.
Small blood vessels are broken, and the ear
becomes swollen and disfigured.   These ear-caps

prove, to a certain extent, safeguards against such accidents.

As we stand waiting in the hall, the captain addresses a few words to us. He is a fine player, and an International himself, so that what he says is worth hearing. A captain who leads his men and explains by example is worth a hundred captains who go behind and shout their directions. "The ground is fairly dry," he says, "though it will probably break up and turn muddy later on, when our feet have churned it up a bit. Anyhow we are strong behind, and I want you to play a loose game. Spread out when you dribble, tackle hard, and when you do heel out, heel out clean. Don't let the ball trickle out of the scrum so that their half gets to it as soon as does our own. That's about all that I've got to say." The drag with its four horses comes rolling up to the door, we jump in, and away we go.

I always used to feel, when driving to the ground in a Yorkshire town, as if I was a member of, say, the " Light Blue troupe of knockabout artistes— for one *matinée* only." On this occasion there is, undoubtedly, a suspicion of the circus about us.

We are perched up on the drag in our conspicuous
club colours, and driven, by what I cannot but
believe to be a most roundabout route, to the
ground. As we pass the whispering groups of
spectators, I instinctively call to mind the proces-
sion which promenades the town of a morning to
advertise the arrival of the show. Every time our
driver cracks his whip he seems to be saying,
" 'Ere they are, gents, as fine a lot of well-growed
young uns as ever you saw. Walk up, walk up ;
they're just a-going to begin." However, we get
to the big gates at last, and pass through a long
avenue of interested, though somewhat grimy, faces
to the pavilion, into whose shady depths we
plunge with a sense of relief.

Then for a quarter of an hour or so we lounge
about, the younger members of the team experi-
encing that indefinable sensation of nervousness
which is described at the Universities as "getting
the needle." We do not go out on to the ground,
for that would spoil the "entrance." The game
is to be partly football, remember, and partly a
knockabout entertainment. Like the circus troupe,
we have the spectators to think of, and as it
would never do for the bare-back rider to practice

his tricks while the gallery was filling, so our agile three-quarters must not "cavort" about the ground until time is up, and the seats are packed with the audience. However, all things come to an end in time, and presently our captain, who has left us, returns with the news that he has won the toss, and that we are playing with the wind. "You must do all you know at first," he says, "and try and hang on afterwards. The wind is strong, but it may fail a bit after half time." A minute later, and our wraps are off; the doors swing open, and we walk on to the field of play.

There we stand, the gladiators of the nineteenth-century colosseum. The great multitude wraps us round with its dark embrace; a silent crowd, some twenty thousand strong, rising tier on tier above us. There is something so business-like in the concentrated stare of those forty thousand eyes, that an ancient Roman, could he be placed amongst them, would probably express surprise that we did not turn to the central stand and cry the "*Morituri te salutant*" to the committee. A young undergraduate, who has never played in the North before, turns to me, half in jest and half in earnest, and says, " I don't like

this, old chap ; I feel as if I couldn't run away ! "
I tell him that I quite agree with him. But our
talk is interrupted by a mighty shout that goes
echoing away into the distance. What is it ?—
ah, the " home " team. Conscious of their popularity, the men come skipping and jumping on to
the field, throwing the ball they bring with them
from one to the other, and playing the practical
jokes which are the average Englishman's idea of
humour. Fifteen strong, square fellows, hard as
nails all of them ; short and dark for the most
part, such as the Yorkshire towns breed—a race
apart from their tall, fair, broad-shouldered brethren
of the dales. Three of them, indeed, are of the
latter class, immense towers of muscle and brawn,
but they are the exception, and quite dwarf their
sturdy companions.

They have the right to kick off, and presently
a tall forward steps from amongst them and
places the ball on the centre line. Our men fall
back into their proper positions. Their forwards
line up and stand like greyhounds—or rather
terriers—in the leash ; there is a cry and an
answering shout from our captain ; the tall forward
takes four short paces, and the ball shoots into

the air as if from a mortar—not a long kick,
perhaps, but high, as a kick-off should be. The
forwards rush up under it at full speed ; the crowd
cheer wildly, as well they may, for has not a game
commenced between two teams of no little repute
in this football world of ours?

It was a near thing. The forwards were almost
upon our wing three-quarter when he caught the
ball. But they had no raw recruit to deal with.
The first and the second man he dodges, and then
punts high into the air. The tables are turned
with a vengeance. The wind catches the ball, and
carries it along toward the opposite goal, while
under it speeds the fleetest foot in Cambridge. A
Yorkshire three-quarter catches the ball, but as
he does so he is hurled over, and the pair roll
on the ground together, while round them swing
the opposing packs of forwards. " Let the men
out," is the cry, and out they both crawl, and trot
quietly back to their places. The ball is rolled by
a half under the arch where the front ranks of the
bending forwards meet, and the scrummage has
commenced. What have I been doing ? Nothing
much up to the present, but now I find myself in
the third row of the swaying mass. We have

managed to get the first shove, which, being interpreted, means that by driving the enemy back we
have obtained the ball. It is now passed back by
the feet of the front rank to the second rank, and I
can see it as I lean in the scrummage just before
me ; so I shove steadily ahead. Are we to heel
out ? No ; we are rather too far from the enemy's
goal-line, our captain thinks, and he gives no sign.
They are holding us now, and we make no head-
way. We must change our tactics, and try to
" screw " them, which, translated from football
dialect, means that we must try and push them off
the ball, so that they will pass by us on the one
side, while we dash on with it at our feet on
the other. " To the right," whispers our leader ;
at the word the men in the front rank begin to
push steadily towards the left, while we behind
shove slightly to our right, keeping the ball in our
midst. The " screw " is, on this occasion at least,
successful. Our opponents, pressed out of the
direct line for the moment, sweep back our front
rank to the left. But the Yorkshiremen have not
got our whole scrummage routed before them as
they think. Quickly we on the right slip by them,
and before the majority can see what has occurred,

five of us are free from the scrummage, which is now in a state of utter confusion, and are away down the field. A half-back makes an ineffectual dash at the ball, but misses it. There are but two opponents immediately before us now—a three-quarter and the full back. Then our leading forward, who has the ball at his feet, loses his head. As the three-quarter comes dashing up, he kicks past him, but, alas! he kicks too hard. In an instant their full-back has pounced upon it, and we rush at him, only to see the ball go sailing over our heads into touch behind our backs. "Awful sorry," grunts the culprit, and we trot back to the touch-line in not the most pleasant frame of mind imaginable.

"Mark your men there!" cries their captain, as we line up in two parallel rows at right angles to the touch-line ; for it is "our ball," and our half will have the right to throw it out to us. Away it flies, fair and true, about half-way down the long line. Our huge Welsh friend leaps at it, and has it in a moment. Will he get through? No; a little Yorkshireman has him round the thighs, and rolls him over as if he were a baby. Round them we sweep, and another scrummage

O

is formed. " Let the backs have a show," whispers
our captain. For a second time we get the ball,
and then those behind straddle their legs an inch
or two wider and out it rolls, propelled by a backward kick, right into the hands of the half
waiting to receive it. Like a flash he is off,
travelling, however, but a few yards before he
transfers it to his companion, who is running on
his right. Away goes number two, taking a
slightly slanting direction, and drawing the tackle
of the three-quarter and half in front of him.
As these two rush at him together, he again
passes the ball. A gap has been left in the
enemy's line of defence, and in an instant our
Scotch three-quarter, who now has the ball, dashes
through. Away he speeds down the field with
a capital start. He has only the back to avoid,
and two of our men are in close attendance on
him in case he should find himself in difficulties.
Out shoots the back, and sends him staggering
to the ground a dozen feet away ; but his effort
though magnificent is vain, for the Scotchman has
thrown the ball to one of his companions, who
runs in and grounds it between the posts.

There is a low murmur in the crowd, and

the light of battle glows in the eyes of the
Yorkshiremen as they walk sullenly into goal, and
line up ready to make a dash at our captain, who
has elected to take the kick himself. A half strolls
out with the ball under his arm, and, turning his
back to the enemy, digs a substantial trench
with his boot-heel. Then he drops flat on the
ground, and holding the ball at arm's length, looks
up at his captain, who stands but two paces away.
"How's that?" he says. "About right," comes
the answer. "No—a bit straighter, I think. That's
it—put it down." The ball is placed in the hole ;
our opponents rush out with a shout ; but it is
all in vain. The ball rises fair and true, passing between the posts about six feet above the
bar. The referee blows his whistle, and back we
trot to the centre line, with a goal to our credit
in the first twelve minutes—not a bad performance that, gentlemen !

But we must look to our laurels. These sturdy
bull-dog men mean business now, and no mistake
about it. A jeer or two is heard from the crowd,
which tokens of contempt they receive with rather
ugly looks. Off flies the ball, and under it race
their forwards upon one of our luckless wing

three-quarters, who stands waiting to receive it. The wind catches the ball, and it hangs in the air. Will it never come down? Yes—at length it falls, but falls too late. The "tykes" are on our man, and over and over he rolls. One of them whips it up and dashes on. But, see, speeding across the ground comes our Scotchman; two of their men are close together. Surely, if the first is tackled, it will avail us little, for he is already preparing to pass the ball to his companion. But no; at his topmost speed—and he has weight as well to back him—the Scotchman takes them *both*, an arm for each, and over go the three in a struggling heap; while we, who are in hot pursuit, swing round behind the ball. Saved this time! Yet we are in our own twenty-five, and perilously near our goal. And now for some fifteen minutes we struggle desperately to guard our lines. Time after time our halves throw themselves on to the ball under the feet of their advancing forwards; time after time our backs perform prodigies of tackling and kicking; but in our twenty-five we are forced to stay, and there we remain till the whistle proclaims that the welcome half-time has arrived.

Out comes a plate of sliced lemon, and many

of us are glad enough to suck the acid juice, for
the work has been of no light order. Our captain
strolls around, looking rather pleased with himself,
but anxious too ; for he knows that the real
struggle has now to come. A few hacks and a
cut or two have been received, but no accident
of a serious nature has yet occurred. The minute
or two of waiting soon passes, and we line up
again for the play. We have the kick-off—against
the wind ; but our captain is not so successful
as the Yorkshiremen were at their last attempt
under similar circumstances. The ball keeps low,
and their centre three-quarter has ample time to
catch and return it with a long kick into touch
before we can reach him.

At the line-out an incident occurs which raises
the wildest enthusiasm amongst the crowding
masses who watch the game. We are not far from
our twenty-five, and so our half-back throws the
ball to a stalwart forward standing but a yard or
two out, who is, however, marked by a still more
stalwart Yorkshireman—one of the men from the
dales that I have mentioned. Our man springs
and catches the ball, but, in the twinkling of an
eye, he is hurled to the ground by his gigantic

opponent with quite unnecessary violence. The
crowd cheer loudly. You must not be surprised
at that. Remember, please, that half of them
have come in the hope of seeing a bit of
" scrappin'," and greet its appearance with all the
enthusiasm displayed by spectators at a cricket
match, when a ball flies out of the ground for
six! But more is yet to come. The ball has
again rolled into touch, and their half-back, out
of pure bravado, drops it again just where the
two frowning combatants are standing. This time
the Yorkshireman receives it, and in an instant
thirteen and a half stone of bone and muscle flies
at him like a cannon-ball. Down he goes with
a crash—as the oak falls to the woodman's axe,
to use a metaphor from friend Virgil. The yells
are deafening ; a hoot or two may be heard,
but the vast majority of the shouting is con-
gratulatory applause. We are strangers from the
South, and since no cup is to be lost or won, and
no betting on the event has taken place, the spectators do not seem to mind very much which
side gets the worst of the rough play. All they
ask is that an occasional bit of the aforesaid
" scrappin' " shall occur—not a very exorbitant

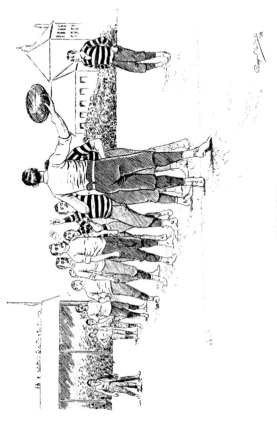

OUT OF TOUCH

demand, after all, as things go nowadays. A collar-bone has snapped, and the injured hero walks off the field nursing his arm, and using language which I am sure he will regret in his calmer moments.

For some time the game sways backwards and forwards, but is, on the whole, of a very even character. At length, however, our forwards begin to slack their work in the scrummage, and slowly we are pushed back, past the half-way line, past the twenty-five line, so that we are almost on our goal-line. Here we pull ourselves together for a desperate stand, and in scrummage after scrummage gain a little ground. But it is our last effort. The ball is heeled out to their half, and our three-quarters dash forward to mark their opponents. Yet the wily half does not pass, but runs himself between the scrummage and the touch-line, and drops over the line amid a roar of cheers from the sea of waving hats and sticks. However, we have not much to fear, for the kick is at a most difficult angle. We watch the half-back carry out the ball, and stand in line like runners ready for a hundred yards' dash. He has put it down! Out we rush; but stay—we

were over-eager—he has done nothing of the
kind. " No charge ! " shouts the referee, and we
have to remain in goal while the half-back
arranges the ball in the hole he has made for
it without further fear of molestation. At last
the kick comes—a mighty one, and well-directed
—but the wind carries the ball aside, and "no
goal" is the cry. " Come on, you men ; play
up ! " says our captain ; and out we run to the
twenty-five, and off goes the ball, spinning through
the air towards our opponents' goal.

Blood is up on both sides now, and the hardest
of tackling and the fiercest of dribbling is in full
progress. Our full back catches the ball, but before
he can kick it he is knocked head over heels,
and slightly sprains his ankle. Another of the
players *hors de combat.* Our opponents have been
playing one man short ; but matters are now
equalized. What is to be done? " Take a forward out of the scrummage," says the captain,
looking rather blankly at us as we stand grouped
around him. " I wish you would let me go back
for a time," says one of the most stalwart of us, six
feet one in his boots, and forty-four inches round
the chest. He is a fine tackle and a fair kick,

but it seems hard to lose him in the scrummage. "It's just this," he continues, dabbing his head sorrowfully with his handkerchief: "I've got a nasty cut in my head, and I'm making a beastly mess of everybody in the scrummage, besides hurting myself infernally every time I go into it." "Oh, very well," says his commander; and the game proceeds.

And now occurs an incident that will never be forgotten by any one who witnessed it. The Yorkshiremen start a beautiful passing run down the field. They are round our scrummage before the forwards know anything about it. By brilliant passing, the ball is carried past our halves and three-quarters, although in so doing the hard tackling grasses all of the runners save one—a burly man, with a great reputation for a decidedly forcible style of play. Our full back was a light man of no particular ability. This our friend the Yorkshireman knows, and forgetting that a change in that position has been effected, he makes no attempt to dodge, but charges straight down on the player before him, trusting that his strength and pace will annihilate him. Our man, nothing loth, meets him in full career. There is a crash as of a railway collision;

without exaggeration it may be heard by the
spectators in the uttermost parts of the field ; "and
still stood all who saw them fall, while men might
count a score ;" then up goes a shout that rends
the listening air.   It was a most gallant tackle,
and there is no one who does not cheer the pair as
they rise, blown it is true, but otherwise none the
worse for the encounter.   Nothing more occurs
till the call of time, and we leave the field winners
by a goal to a try.

Such is a short account of a Rugby Union
football match as it would be played under modern
rules in the year 1896.   Perhaps I have been
unfortunate in describing a game in which two
accidents occur.   To those who know little of
football I will, therefore, say that for two to take
place in one match is a most unusual occurrence.
That the scene could scarcely be laid in a Yorkshire club ground is a fact unfortunately true since
the formation of the Northern League.   But such
a battle could have occurred in that great football
county not so very long ago, when disunion was
not thought of as a matter of " practical politics."

CHAPTER XIII.

HINTS TO THOSE IN AUTHORITY IN ENGLISH
SCHOOLS.

"PORT," once wrote Whyte Melville, "rouses manly qualities of body and mind, excites intellectual faculties and muscular powers, braces the nervous system, and stimulates arm, heart, and brain to healthful effort. Few true sportsmen but are frank of nature, kindly and generous." So a great sportsman summed up the advantages of sport. Rugby football can be included in the term, for all athletics are forms of sport, and football is, in my opinion at least, the finest form of athletics. Its value in schools is immense; its superiority over other games marked. Cricket

does not provide the safety-valve for youthful
energy that is to be found in Rugby football ;
rowing may easily strain a weak heart if racing
is indulged in too early in life ; no other games
can be played regularly every day, and yet
excite the interest and provide the exercise that
is to be found in Rugby football. Yet at first
many schoolmasters, sharing the prejudiced opinions
of the boys' parents, objected to the game.   It
was considered rough and ungentlemanly.   The
Brighton Academy, where poor little Dombey
dragged out his weary existence under the tutel-
age of Dr. Blimber, was the type of many of the
old schools.   The exercise was limited to walks
after the fashion of the "crocodile" in the modern
girls' school.   Now the smallest schools in the
kingdom have football and cricket teams, which
are considered just as much a part of their
educational system as Latin and mathematics.

As its name denotes, Rugby football had its
origin in Rugby School.   To the history of its
development at Rugby and other public schools,
I will refer in another chapter.   All I now
wish to point out is that Rugby football sprang
from the schools.   Many years elapsed before it

found favour with the working classes, who in many places were already playing some rough form of game, which they designated football for want of a better name. Gradually these working classes have made the game their own, so that, in the North of England at any rate, they have almost crushed out the gentleman amateur. Into the causes that brought about this unfortunate condition of affairs I will not inquire; they have already been discussed in the present book. But as the great North-country clubs, that have in the past supplied so many of the most famous International players, gradually are sucked into the professional vortex, so will the public schools rise in importance. It is to them that we shall have to look to maintain the purity and high traditions of the great game. In their hands will be the training of the men who are to represent England in its battles with what Lord Salisbury has called the "Celtic Fringe." They will be the nurseries of future Internationals.

It is thus very necessary that the game that is taught at schools should be a sound and correct game if England wishes to keep up her football reputation. To do this requires constant attention

from the elder boys and from those masters who
are themselves skilled in the game. An excellent
practice has sprung up within the last few years
of demanding from a master skill in games as well
as mental ability. It was discovered that the most
distinguished University scholars were often value-
less as teachers. They had neither the power to
command successfully, nor the strength of character, to enforce obedience to the orders they
gave. Boys will cheerfully obey the celebrated
"blue" who has won for himself a great reputation ;
for amongst boys hero-worship, and especially
athletic hero-worship, flourishes exceedingly. His
power for good is therefore immense, for they will
follow his footsteps with an alacrity, and listen to
his advice with a respect that no dignitary of the
Church, preach he never so wisely, could command.
There is no reason, as Whyte Melville has told
us, why *mens* and *moles* should not be combined.
C. B. Fry, the Oxonian, has proved that he possesses great ability ; C. M. Wells, of Cambridge,
was a first-class classic ; Adie, the light blue oars-
man, was a Senior Wrangler. These are facts
which the heads of the public schools have fully
appreciated. There is no doubt that the influence

of athletic masters has invariably been for good, both on the physical and moral welfare of the boys entrusted to their care.

It is an established fact that the Scotch schools turn out finer teams than their English rivals. We find cases where boys, while still at school, played for Scotland for two years in succession. We see, again, that the Scotch boys who go up to Cambridge or Oxford meet with a far larger portion of football success than their brothers of England. Old Fettesians and Old Lorettonians, during the last ten years, have obtained their "blues" in larger numbers than have the boys from any two schools on this side of the border. Yet their joint numbers amount but to some three hundred and thirty boys all told. It is always said at the 'Varsities that a man who turns out in a pair of red stockings—the Fettesian-Lorettonian colours—will certainly be tried for his University, and will in all probability obtain his "blue." What, then, is the reason of this? Why are the Scotch schools so much more successful in training the young idea than our great English colleges? It is a difficult question to answer, but the high standard of football in Scotch schools is, in my

opinion, mainly to be accounted for by the enthusiasm aroused by the inter-school competitions,
in which Fettes and Loretto, Blair Lodge and
Merchiston, fight out an annual championship.

English head-masters have always been rather
afraid of inter-school matches. They seem to
imagine that the necessary keenness to win will
lead to innumerable cases of rough play. I do
not think that there is the slightest chance of such
untoward events occurring. Take, as an example,
the Scotch competitions, which have always been
marked by the most honest and sportsmanlike
play. In the Inter-University match, again, there
is never a suspicion of what the Americans call
" slogging " (which is quite distinct from hard
tackling) ; and, after all, undergraduates are but
schoolboys in disguise. Under the old style of
play, indeed, with its hacking and tripping, matters
were very different. The annual match between
Clifton and Marlborough under the old Rugby
rules, was found to be degenerating into a hacking
bout, and had to be abandoned. But *tempora
mutantur et nos mutamur in illis.* There is no
danger under the present altered circumstances
of a repetition of such unfortunate scandals.

Wellington and Marlborough, Cheltenham and Haileybury, Cheltenham and Rugby, Rugby and Marlborough, and many other schools, now play annual matches, which are in every respect distinct successes. Why, then, should not a regular competition be instituted? The boys cannot be more anxious to win than they now are, and if they play a sportsmanlike game in the present, they can surely be trusted to do the same throughout an inter-school competition in the future.

Mr. C. J. N. Fleming, in his chapter on the Nurseries of football in Scotland, has spoken of the points in temperament and build, which will show to the observer whether or no a boy has the makings of a football player in him. I will not, therefore, touch on this aspect of the question, but rather give a few hints on the best method of teaching a strong and willing boy the game.

Take a young forward, for instance. It is not much good to tell him simply to push for all he is worth when he enters a scrummage, and walk after him with a stick to see that he does so. Tell him to get his head down properly, and then to look for the ball. When he sees it in front of him he can push as hard as he likes. To be "on the

P

ball " is the first requisite of a good forward ; and
this must be impressed upon him.   To work
hard, to break away quickly from the scrummage,
to tackle his opponents with a rush—in short, to
play the old, hard forward game, is what he must
be taught.   Afterwards he can be instructed in
" wheeling," and " screwing," and " winging," and
" heeling out," and the other tricks of the trade
which lighten the work of the men in the scrummage, and give a young and not very keen player
countless opportunities of shirking his duty.   Teach
him to pass and dribble by constant practice in
those accomplishments.   An occasional afternoon's
Association football, with a Rugby ball instead of
a round one, is an excellent method of teaching
the dribbling game to young forwards.   The
famous Welsh clubs believe in it, and practice
this hybrid game for half an hour or so once or
twice during the week.

Many players declare that the success of the
modern passing is due to the fact that the tackling
of forwards and backs alike is neither so hard nor
so keen as in the days gone by.   Our cousins across
the sea declare that an American team would
break up our finest combination by their hard

INTERCEPTING A PASS

tackling. The success of our passing is solely
to be accounted for by the slowness of the men in
getting into play. "It is well enough," one of them
writes, " to be able to pass the ball from one three-
quarter to another if there is only one opponent
who has been fast enough to closely follow it ; but
I need not tell American University men that such
a condition in the game could not exist with our
football players, for with their rapidity of getting
into play every one of those three-quarter backs
would certainly have down on him one determined
tackler, who would not be likely to give the back
a chance to pass the ball. The slowness (as compared to our game), therefore, of the men getting
into play I consider to explain why the passing
is so successful in the Rugby Union game." There
is much in what he says. Teach the forwards
to break away quickly from the scrummage, and
teach backs and forwards alike to " down " their
men. Let there be no scrambling on, and half-
hearted tackling, which is worse than useless.

One other point is worthy of mention. Be
careful to coach the team in place and drop-
kicking. When players leave school they have
little or no time, unless they enter one of the

Universities, to practise these most effective accomplishments. I should strongly advise all school authorities to found competitions for place and drop-kicking, and to see that the number of entries in them is large. Accurate kicking is declining every year, and it is the duty of the schools to see that the evil does not spread further. Let the boys learn it at school, or they will never learn it at all.

I agree with Mr. Marshall, who stated, in a recent article published in the "Football Handbook," that "amongst boys the encouraging of individual play is what is required." Take, for instance, a lad who has all the makings of a fine half-back, a lad who can get away like lightning with the ball, and can pass swiftly and surely. Suppose that the captain of the school team is a selfish three-quarter with indifferent pace, he may insist, for what he calls the benefit of " combination," on the half passing to him on every possible and impossible occasion. Indeed, he may check and spoil his game in a hundred ways. It is the same with a three-quarter, who might turn into a dodgy runner of remarkable ability, but is thwarted by continual orders to pass the ball. Neither a half nor a three-quarter is a mere conduit pipe, whatever theorists may say on the matter. Let the boys develop each his individual game at school as long as they keep within the recognized limits of honest, hard-working, unselfish football ; and let those in authority over them leave the final polish to the University or the first-class club. This may seem a hard saying, but as a matter of fact schoolboy players will, if individually brilliant, combine naturally into a formidable team. What I mean is, that manufacturing fine individual athletes is better than winning school matches by what I may describe as precocious combination.

It is obvious that football is of the greatest assistance to a schoolmaster in teaching the boys to love the fresh air, to desire to keep fit and well rather than to go smoking surreptitiously under neighbouring haystacks, and to regard with contempt the flabby youths who hang around the inevitable "tuck-shop." It has, of course, its disadvantages. One accident will set a crowd of fanatics howling. As I have stated elsewhere, it is not a dangerous game ; but fanatics are impervious to reason. On one point, however, I would insist. Make the game compulsory if you

like, play it as often as you like, but see that each
boy is examined by a medical man. There is
nothing gained by endangering heart or lungs, if
either are at all in a doubtful condition. This
examination is all the more necessary, as the game
grows faster every year, and with a faster game
comes a greater strain on the organs I have
mentioned.

To encourage *esprit de corps* amongst the boys
is most important. To be keen on the success of
the school is, however, one thing, and to neglect
the game itself in order to watch the doings of
the first fifteen is another. The growing tendency
amongst boys to delight in acting as spectators
rather than players must be vigorously checked.
Now and again exceptions may be made when
one of the great school matches of the season
is in progress ; but, generally speaking, each boy
should take his own regular exercise every day,
and not spend his time strolling about and
applauding the exertions of others.

Masters should do everything in their power to
assist the school captain to coach his men. At
the same time I am strongly opposed to any
interference on their part in the selection of the

teams, as grievances spring up so easily under such circumstances. Yet they can give friendly advice, and, should they be men with great football reputations, this advice will in all probability be readily listened to by the boys. One thing, above all! Let there be no "favouritism" by the boy, or boys, who select the team. I do not think that in the larger schools there is much danger of it, for public opinion is too strong ; but in the smaller schools the danger is not inconsiderable. Remember, ye captains, as I have said in a previous chapter on you and your ways, favouritism is fatal! The team take sides, the injured boys grumble in corners, the favoured one is shamefaced, and then good-bye to all good-fellowship and *esprit de corps*.

House matches are an absolute necessity in big schools in England where the number of "foreign" matches is limited. They alone will keep up the necessary keenness for the game, which otherwise may tend to disappear. I do not believe in compelling the boys to play too many times a week. It may have a similar effect to the lack of house matches in causing the boys to grow tired of the game. Three times a week is, in my opinion,

sufficient. On other days let them practise kicking and passing, if they like, or, still better, try
some other form of exercise. The volunteers may
drill, or runs across country be organized. In the
gymnasium I put great faith. The first physical
qualities necessary for a football player are lithe-
ness and activity, combined with strength. A
series of light gymnastics will give a boy a chance
to develop the qualities required. Boxing, fencing,
and wrestling are also of assistance ; they teach
the hand to obey the eye. All feats of strength,
such as weight-lifting, should be avoided by boys.
They run considerable risk of straining themselves
and, in addition to this, such exercise stiffens the
muscles, so that what a boy may gain in strength
he must lose in activity.

An interesting article has recently appeared in
the *Daily News*, on the scholarship and athletic
records of public schools. I should advise the
opponents of Rugby football in schools to note the
quotations I shall extract from it. The materials for
the article were supplied by the head-masters themselves, and it can thus be safely assumed that they
are correct. " In passing into the Campus Martius,"
says the writer, " are we leaving the scholarship

winners behind, and will none of them be winners of future Waterloos? With a view to settle that question, we asked the head-masters to be so kind as to state whether the boys were athletes ; whether, in particular, they were members of the cricket or football teams. We had expected to find this very rare. What with over-pressure and over-work, the fierce competition, the bait, the bribes, we thought it impossible. But, in fact, we constantly find that these scholars elect are in the school eleven or fifteen, or if not are athletes of other kinds. It is quite common to find both the cricket and the football captain in the scholarship list. In fact, the schoolmaster seems quite as proud of the athletic as of the scholastic feats. We hear of a batting average of forty ; of a Balliol scholar being at once captain of cricket and football; of a Trinity scholar who ' is the best forward in our school team, and runs the mile well under 4·50 on grass ;' and of a Corpus (Oxford) scholar who 'was in the football fifteen, and won the open quarter in fifty-three seconds.' Putting the information we have received together, we find that about 40 per cent. of these scholars are in one or other of the two teams. And it is not only in the large schools where the scholars are also athletes, but is rather the other way. If we take only the schools which win one or two scholarships, we find the percentage rises to 60. A curious contrast is the following : Both Rugby and Bradford get seven scholarships. No one at Rugby is in either team ; all the seven at Bradford are."

Such is my answer to those who would have us believe that if an attempt is made to develop matter as well as mind, the former must obtain complete mastery over the latter.

I cannot conclude this chapter without one further quotation, from an article by Dr. Almond, the father of Scotch football. Of football in schools he writes : "It is perhaps, under all modern circumstances, their best instrument of 'education' in the true and wide sense of the word ; for I cannot conceive of any school making a good stand-up fight against the soft and indulgent ways of living in which town boys, at all events of the richer classes, are usually brought up, in which football is not a flourishing institution."

CHAPTER XIV.

THE NURSERIES OF FOOTBALL IN ENGLAND.

ONE of the proudest boasts of every Englishman should be the English public school. Without wishing to rival the exaggerated platitudes of a continental patriot, I think I may safely assert that no system of education has been so successful as our own in turning out honest, well-mannered gentlemen. Young men often explain the bad temper, the inability to stand "chaff," or the social *faux pas* of a companion by the remark, "You see, he was never at a public school." What, then, is the reason of this? It is due in a great measure to the popularity of manly games, such as football

and cricket. To be a fine athlete, a boy must be
plucky, he must practise self-denial, he must learn
to keep his temper, and, above all, he must possess
the Anglo-Saxon bulldog endurance which has
done so much for England in the past. There is
another point worthy of notice : despite the intense
athletic hero-worship in schools, it is a rare thing
to find a really distinguished boy cricketer or
footballer who, in schoolboy parlance, "fancies
himself." It is the mediocre player who "puts
on side." The great athlete is usually a quiet,
modest young fellow, disinclined to orate on the
subjects of his own achievements. There are, of
course, black sheep in every school ; but if loafers
and snobs and tuft-hunters are to be met with
amongst boys, they cannot be said to be so popular
or to be so well received as in the great world
outside. In the majority of these little republics
the highest and most manly ideals prevail, and, in
my humble opinion, athletics have had much to
do with putting these ideals upon their pedestals.
Whatever those worthies may say who think that
to win a fat scholarship is the end and object of
school life, it seems to me that the making of
honest English gentlemen is of infinitely more

importance ; boys who delight in the great deeds of their chosen heroes are stages above the members of our modern society who appear to think only of the money-bags of their millionaires. The qualities we all admire in the schoolboy hero are conspicuous by their absence in the character of the latter much-worshipped individual.

It seems almost a pity that the English schools are so divided in their allegiance to the various forms of football. But so they are, and so it seems they must ever remain. There is the Rugby football group, with Rugby, Cheltenham, Haileybury, Clifton, Marlborough, Wellington, Tonbridge, and a host of others ; there is the Association group, amongst whom Charterhouse, Westminster, Repton, and Shrewsbury stand conspicuous. Lastly, there is a small group of schools each of which play a different game of football ; amongst them are Eton, Harrow, Winchester, and, until the last few years, Shrewsbury, Charterhouse, and Westminster. The games developed by this group were, there is little doubt, originally intended to suit the capacities of their individual playgrounds. It must be remembered that the great playing fields, without which a modern public school can hardly be imagined, are in the majority of cases quite modern.

It is not my purpose to speak at any great length of these varying forms of football, for this is a Rugby football book, and should deal with Rugby football schools. At Eton, as every one knows, there are two styles of football played—the one termed the "wall," and the other the "field" game. The "wall" game, as its name denotes, is played against the wall, about eight feet high, of the Slough to Windsor road. To the uninitiated it can scarcely be said to appear very attractive. Its origin was probably the passage football, which most schoolboys play, in defiance of authority, in study and dormitory passages. The goals are—on the one side a door, and on the other the marked trunk of a large elm, neither of which are within the field of play. The players are eleven a side, and three of their number who come in frequent contact with the walls are protected by "sacks," or, in other words, padded sweaters and caps, which protect the head and ears. The "field" game is played on a field about a hundred and twenty yards long, and ninety yards wide. Without going into details, I may mention that it is a dribbling game, but, as in Rugby football, the off-side rule is enforced. The majority of Etonians, who are keen on football, play the Association game on leaving school, and the excellent teams turned out by the Old Etonians bear witness to the value of the Eton " field " game in teaching dribbling and kicking.

The Harrow game is also of ancient extraction. It differs from both Rugby and Association, in that the ball may be handled, but only when it is kicked from below the knee, and caught by another player before it touches the ground. The cry of " Yards " is then called, and the catcher may run three yards, and drop, punt, or dribble it. No player may be tackled. The game further differs from Association in possessing an absolute off-side rule.

The Winchester game is of a somewhat complicated nature. The ground is blockaded on one side by a netting about ten feet high, to keep the ball within proper limits. This is, in reality, an innovation, for the old custom was to plant a line of "fags" outside the ropes on that side to recover the ball when it was sent out of bounds. The "hot," which is a form of

scrummage, is very like the old Rugby football
scrummages of the seventies, being a hard, pushing match. The ball must be kicked as hard as
possible ; there is no dribbling as in Association.
No passing is allowed, nor off-side play, which is
penalized by a " hot." Matches of twenty-two,
fifteen, and six a side are played.

The Shrewsbury and Westminster games closely
approached Association, and only a slight change
was necessary when the school authorities decided
to adopt that game. " Dowling," as the old
Shrewsbury game was called, differed from Association mainly in allowing a fair catch to be
made, to be followed by a punt. The off-side rule
was also enforced. Neither running with the ball
nor tackling were allowed. It was, in my opinion,
very wise of these schools to accept the Association
rules. While granting that these various forms of
football require skill and afford exercise, a young
man, nevertheless, finds himself in a most unpleasant position when on leaving school he is
confronted with the fact that he must either
give up football altogether, or learn a new game.
Either at a University, should he enter one, or
in any profession that he may choose to adopt,

he will, of course, find that there are many other forms of athletics which he can select for a recreation; yet for a man who is thoroughly devoted to football this can scarcely be described as an adequate consolation.

I will now shake off this Association dust from my feet, and turn to the Rugby schools, the *fons et origo* of the Rugby football game in England, as they have well been called.

RUGBY SCHOOL! First by right of title, at least, amongst all competitors. Few men exist, I should imagine, who have not, as boys, revelled in "Tom Brown's Schooldays," that immortal book from the pen of the late Judge Hughes. In our time we must all have found a hero in the great Pater Brooke; we must all have laughed at Crab Jones, with his straw in his mouth, the "coolest, queerest fish in Rugby;" we must all have echoed in our hearts the "bravos" that greeted the charge of little East, an *alias* that, so rumour tells, hid the boy whose name, during the wildest times of the wild mutiny, was to become another word for reckless valour throughout the length and breadth of India. There are, I have always maintained, few more stirring pieces of

Q

descriptive writing than that which tells of the
last charge of the school-house at the end of the
long football fray. It was not the football that
we know, but it was, as Judge Hughes wrote, something " worth living for." As we read we can picture that advancing mass, one hundred and twenty
strong ; " reckless of the defence of their own goal,
on they come across the level Bigside ground, the
ball well down amongst them, straight for our
goal, like the column of the Old Guard up the
slope at Waterloo. All former charges have been
child's play to this. Warner and Hodge have met
them, but still on they come. The bulldogs rush
in for the last time ; they are hurled over, or
carried back, striving foot, hand, and eyelids. Old
Brooke comes sweeping round the skirts of the
play, and, turning short round, picks out the very
heart of the scrummage, and plunges in. It
wavers for a moment—he has the ball. No, it
has passed him, and his voice rings out clear
over the advancing tide, ' Look out in goal ! '
Crab Jones catches it for a moment, but before
he can kick the rush is upon him, and passes over
him ; and he picks himself up behind them with
his straw in his mouth, a little dirtier, but as cool

FORMING A SCRUMMAGE

as ever." And so the stirring tale runs on, until
the præposter in goal saves the try by touching the
ball down, and Tom gets all the wind knocked out
of his small body by the avalanche of rushing
forwards. Hacking there may have been in those
days, hacking which we in our sober senses must
admit was often of a cruel, almost brutal nature ;
but there is no one with true English blood in his
veins who cannot, after reading the whole of that
famous chapter, realize the wild delight in the
exercise of strength and endurance and skill which
fascinates the players of Rugby football as much
to-day as in the time that Judge Hughes wrote of
more than sixty years ago. "The whole sum of
schoolboy existence gathered up into one straining,
struggling half-hour, a half-hour worth a year of
common life."

It was from Rugby that the game spread,
carried by Old Rugbeans to other schools where
they went as masters, or to clubs which they
founded to keep alive the game they had learnt
to love at school. Rugby and Marlborough supplied three-fourths of the famous players of the
sixties. In 1865 Old Rugbeans and Old Marlburians formed the entire Richmond team — a

team which did not suffer a single defeat. After
the foundation of the Rugby Union the first
five presidents were all Old Rugby boys. The
new rules of that body differed to a certain
extent from those of the old school. Hacking
and tripping were abolished ; the ball was to
be thrown back into the field of play from
the spot where it entered touch ; lastly, the complicated rules which governed the bringing out
of the ball after a try had been obtained, and
before the kick at goal was attempted—for a
description of which go to " Tom Brown " again—
were done away with.

It was not until 1890 that the school accepted
the Rugby Union rules *en bloc.* Hacking died
hard. An Old Rugbean once told me that schoolboy disputes were often settled by an appeal to
shin-kicking. The method was somewhat the same
as that adopted, according to the traveller's tale,
by the South Sea Islanders, who have alternate
whacks at each other's heads with stout cudgels
until one owns himself vanquished. The famous
footballer, Mr. Arthur Guillemard, has mentioned
a tradition which " points to a notable match for
the honours of ' Cock House ' some thirty years

ago, when the losing twenty were so severely punished forward, that their house-master actually sat down on the grass in touch and cried like a child." However, as Molière's doctor remarked, "*nous avons changé tout cela!*" both at Rugby School and in the Rugby Union. It was due to the keenness of Old Rugby boys that the game found its way to the Universities. At Oxford one of the original rules of the club was that the captain, secretary, and at least one of the three committeemen must be a Rugbean. This rule remained unaltered for seven years. At Cambridge an attempt was made to blend the Eton, Harrow, and Rugby games under one code of rules. The result was, however, by no means satisfactory, and the games separated never to meet again.

At the present moment Rugby, under the Rev. H. A. James, has about 550 boys on its books. The keenness for football is well maintained, both by outside matches and the competition between the various houses for the proud position of " Cock House." There is no special training as regards diet. J. J. Dobie, who was captain in 1895, writes to me stating that he considers training as far as food is concerned quite unnecessary at school. Fixed meals and the rules forbidding smoking practically insure good training. At the beginning of the season he believes in cross-country runs, which get the men into hard condition.

The boys play on half-holidays—that is, on Tuesdays, Thursdays, and Saturdays. On every third Monday there is an additional half-holiday, so that in ordinary weeks they play three times, but in every third week four times. "Big side," which consists of two teams picked by the captain from all the houses, which are ten in number, is played twice a week. Those boys who are not playing on "Big side" have sides made up for them by their house captains. Each house has a first and second team, exclusive of the "Big side" players, and matches are arranged between them while "Big side" is going on. On the half-holiday on which "Big side" is not played the rounds in the competition for the position of "Cock House," between the full first fifteens of the ten houses, are fought out. In these matches the referee must be a member of the first fifteen of the school, and his selection is the result of an arrangement between the captains of the two competing teams. "Little sides" are also arranged between the smaller boys in the various houses.

Mr. H. C. Bradby has rendered invaluable service to the football at Rugby. Matches between the first fifteen and the next twenty-two, or the first fifteen and the masters, are arranged, and during their progress he coaches the school players, stopping the game and pointing out faults when necessary. As he also referees in "foreign" matches, he is able to render informal assistance to the captain of the fifteen in the selection of the players. The captain and secretary this year are united in the person of H. G. Pearson.

After Rugby, MARLBOROUGH is more closely associated with the early history of the game than any other school. As I have already stated, the Richmond team in the sixties was often entirely composed of past members of the two schools. At Oxford and Cambridge Old Rugbeans and Old Marlburians worked hand in hand to secure a firm footing for the game. In 1872 four Old Marlburians were included in the team that played against Scotland. The Marlborough Nomads were among the original clubs which joined the Rugby Union in 1871.

Marlborough at the present time, under the Rev. G. C. Bell, is in a most flourishing condition, with some 600 boys on its books. It has never waivered in its allegiance to the Rugby game, and the famous Blues and Internationals which it has produced are legion. Amongst them I feel that I am bound to mention Harry Vassall, the celebrated captain of the celebrated Oxford team, which, with its passing system, revolutionized the game as played throughout the football world.

The boys are expected to take steady exercise every day. On four days a week football is played, and on the other two days a two-mile run is compulsory for all. The interest in football is well maintained by a cup, which is competed for every year by the nine houses into which the school is broken up. The winning house fifteen is allowed to wear their house crest on their caps—a much-coveted distinction. Each house has an upper and lower game on football days, and the boys from each house not included in these teams are combined, and display their energies in a "pick up," which is dignified by the name of " Remnants." As there is not sufficient room in the playing-fields for these upper and lower games to be in progress at the same time, the upper games are played in the first hour after dinner, that is to say, between 2.30 and 3.30, and the lower games take place subsequently between 3.30 and 4.30. The respective house captains keep an eye on these lower games to see that there is "no slacking" amongst the boys that are learning their football therein.

To discover the individual merits of the best players, "Big sides" are arranged. In these the school fifteen is equally divided, and the remaining places filled from the ranks of the second fifteen. Valuable assistance in coaching the boys is rendered by Mr. C. H. Wood. The team in 1895, under M. B. Scott, had a fairly successful season. The two chief school matches of the year are those played against Wellington and Clifton. Wellington was defeated, but Clifton, who had an excellent fifteen, were victorious, chiefly through the brilliant play of W. N. Pilkington at three-quarters. G. H. Adams combines the offices of captain and secretary for the season of 1896–7.

Amongst the first clubs that joined the Rugby Union on its foundation we find the name of

WELLINGTON COLLEGE, and for that reason I give
it the third place on my list. Wellington College
has risen in numbers to about 450 boys, under the
Rev. B. Pollock. It was celebrated in the seventies
as a great football school, and Old Wellingtonians
were amongst the strongest supporters of the
game, both at Oxford and Cambridge. Amongst
the distinguished players it produced in those
early times were F. R. Adams, of Richmond (who
played in no less than seven International matches),
M. W. Marshall, and the Hon. H. Laurence.

Football is not played so frequently at Wellington
as at some other schools, and on the whole I think
this is wise. Boys are apt to get stale and tired
of a game that becomes monotonous in its daily
regularity. The whole school plays twice a week,
and once a week the house matches for the usual
house cup are fought out. Some 390 boys are
on the regular playing lists. Masters join in the
school games, and render valuable assistance in
coaching the teams. The match of the year at
Wellington is that against Marlborough. In
1895 Marlborough were victorious, beating Wellington on their own ground for the first time since
the inter-school match was a recognized fixture.

H. M. Davies was captain during the Christmas term of 1895, and A. W. White took his place as captain for the following Lent Term.

CHELTENHAM COLLEGE is another famous Rugby football school. There are about 580 boys there, under the head-mastership of the Rev. R. S. de C. Laffan. The famous players who have learned their football at Cheltenham are too numerous to mention with any particularity. It is worthy of note, however, that the year 1880, when A. J. Forrest, McEwan and Crawford left Cheltenham for Ireland, has been called the "turning year" in the football of that "disthressful nation." After a heavy defeat in 1881, the Irishmen were able to make a draw of the English match in 1882 —a draw, too, considerably in their favour.

Like the other schools I have mentioned, Cheltenham possesses a house challenge cup, which is the subject of an annual competition. In addition to this, the school has a junior challenge cup for the house second fifteens. This is a system worthy of adoption by those schools where it is not already in operation. It teaches the game to the younger boys, and puts additional keenness into their play. At Cheltenham the

captains of the first house fifteens, whenever an
opportunity occurs, watch these second teams, and
coach them up to a proper standard.

From the house first fifteens the captain of the
college team chooses men to play in the college
"pick ups." In these games the college fifteen
meets the next twenty, or scratch teams including
the masters. There are three of these "pick ups"
each week—that is to say, on Mondays, Wed-
nesdays, and Saturdays. On Tuesday and Friday
there are the house matches to be decided for the
cup. Thursday is usually an off-day, but if the
captain of a house thinks that his house second
fifteen have been "slacking," or that a game
would be of advantage to them for the sake of
the additional practice, he makes up two scratch
teams out of his own house.

Cheltenham boys have many opportunities
afforded them of learning good football. The
school has matches with Oxford teams on the
one side, and the South Wales clubs on the other.
In 1895, for instance, Newport A and Cardiff A
sent over strong teams early in the season. Oriel
and Trinity Colleges were met in February.

The first fifteen go to the gymnasium for regular

exercise every evening during the winter months. Dumb-bell and Indian-club exercises last for about an hour. In the coaching of the team, Mr. H. V. Page, Mr. E. Scot-Skirving, and Mr. G. G. Pruen, render valuable assistance. These masters take a great deal of interest in the game, and to them is due much of the success that has followed Cheltenham football during late years. Rugby and Haileybury, the two great inter-school matches of the season, were both won by the Cheltenham boys in 1895. Talbot and Dick Cunyngham amongst the forwards, and Bateman-Champain outside, were the mainstay of the team.

Cheltenham is, as every one probably knows, a great army school. In 1895, for instance, no less than seventeen cadets at Woolwich had passed direct from Cheltenham. The standard of age is high, and there are plenty of boys of eighteen in the school who are invaluable on the football field. B. W. Talbot, who captained the team in 1895 with great success, in a letter speaking of the prowess of the college, writes, " We have never yet been beaten by any school. We are never going to be if we can help it." I think he probably prophesies correctly. *Labor omnia vincit* is the college motto, and Cheltenham boys seem to apply it as much to hard work in the scrummage, as to hard work in the army classes.

"When I played as a schoolboy at CLIFTON," writes Mr. Arthur Budd in Mr. Marshall's excellent history of Rugby football, "the number of players was twenty a-side in an ordinary match, and in the Sixth and school game the latter were allowed forty to the twenty of their sturdier seniors." "Hacking over," he says later, "was permissible, and tripping over a runner was quite as much practised as tackling. A player who could not take and give hacks was not considered worth his salt, and to put one's head down in a scrummage was regarded as an act of high treason. We were frequently boxed in a scrummage for three or four minutes together, only to discover that the half-back had by that time absconded with the ball to the other side of the ground." The rapid change from irresponsible irregularity to combined co-operation has indeed been astonishing.

The captain of the school at Clifton is *ex-officio* captain and secretary of the team. To many schoolboys this system will appear strange, but it has worked and is working well at Clifton. When it happens that the head of the school is physically incapable of playing football, or not good enough to figure in the first fifteen, the member of the team who is highest in "call over" amongst the Sixth Form captains the school in the field. Thus R. V. Vernon was captain in 1894, but as he did not play in foreign matches, J. T. Whitty was captain in the field. L. B. Fyffe was captain in 1895, but A. M. Simpson captained in the field.

No regular coaching is given, but the houses play regularly amongst themselves, and the masters, who umpire, do a good deal of incidental coaching. Amongst them Mr. W. W. Vaughan, the Old Oxford blue, is especially worthy of mention for his exertions in this respect. There are school games on Thursday and Saturday afternoons, consisting of two "Big sides," one "Middle side," and six "Little sides"—nine games in all. Each house plays house "Little sides" twice a week after morning school. During the term the first fifteens of the various houses play seven rounds in a cup competition, and the second fifteens play ten rounds. The former are decided on Tuesday half-holidays, specially given for the purpose. The latter take place once a week. The only school played last season was Marlborough, and Clifton won the match.

"As you have doubtless gathered," L. B. Fyffe writes to me, "house football is the foundation of all Clifton football. The object of our system is not to turn out a first-rate fifteen so much as to ensure a thoroughly high level of football all through the school. I do not know how it strikes the outside observer, but it has answered excellently, and is dear to all Old and Present Cliftonians who are keen on the game."

It is interesting to notice that, like its great rival Cheltenham, Clifton has great success as an army school. In 1895, of the cadets then in Woolwich twelve were from Clifton, to the seventeen from Cheltenham; but of the Sandhurst cadets Clifton had supplied no less than seventeen, to the seven of Cheltenham.

HAILEYBURY has been the football nursery of many famous players, and can reckon amongst them E. T. Gurdon, and his brother Charles. It was in 1878 that E. T. Gurdon first appeared for England. He subsequently played no fewer than seven times against Scotland, five times against Ireland, and four times against Wales. He is universally considered to have been one of the best forwards that ever represented England. Charles was the taller and heavier of the two. He played six times against Scotland, five times against Ireland, and three times against Wales. He was never, however, quite so brilliant as his famous brother.

At the present time Haileybury, under the head-mastership of the Hon. and Rev. Edward Lyttelton, is composed of some 400 boys. The system of training and the arrangement of the school games are the same as those in vogue at Rugby. "Big side" consists of the best thirty players; new players are introduced into it as soon as they have proved their ability in the junior games. "Little side" is the generic term for all the remaining boys, who, during "Big side," play inter-house matches. There is also an inter-house competition, when "Big side" players join in and make the teams fully representative. There are eleven houses, and each house has a first, second, and third fifteen. Everybody in the school plays three times in each week.

Whenever it is possible members of the college fifteen take charge of the "Little side" games, doing what coaching they can. Mr. C. E. Hawkins

R

has proved of great assistance in coaching "Big side," and the well-known Oxford blue, R. H. Cattell, who is an Old Haileybury boy, has done much to help him. Last season was not quite satisfactory as regards the winning of matches. In the inter-school contests between Haileybury on the one side, and Bedford Grammar School, Cheltenham and St. Paul's on the other, the Haileybury team suffered defeat on each occasion, but won the match against Dulwich. N. S. A. Harrison will captain the fifteen during the 1896-7 season, taking the reins of office from J. F. Carter.

Rugby football was introduced into TONBRIDGE SCHOOL early in the sixties. The rules were very much the same as those in use at Rugby School itself. In 1873 Tonbridge followed the excellent example set by Wellington, and joined the Rugby Union. Old Tonbridge boys were of great assistance in the formation of clubs at both Oxford and Cambridge. In 1882, for instance, no less than four of the Light Blue fifteen hailed from the school.

At the present time there are some 440 boys at Tonbridge, under the Rev. Dr. Wood, as headmaster. The first two fifteens play regular games

two or three times a week, but scrummaging and
passing are regularly practised nearly every day.
There is a system of league games, which are
played by all the school, with the exception of
the first and second fifteens. The masters have
always been very keen in coaching the teams,
and giving general advice. Mr. R. L. Aston, the
celebrated Light Blue International three-quarter,
has done much to raise the standard of play
throughout the school. Under his careful teaching,
Tonbridge boys have had every opportunity of
learning sound football.

The chief inter-school matches are those against
Dulwich, St. Paul's and Sherborne. During a
period extending from 1874 to 1895, Dulwich has
been beaten ten times, and has won fifteen times,
while six matches have been drawn. From 1890
to 1895 St. Paul's has been beaten three times, and
has won three times. Sherborne was played for
the first time in 1895, and suffered defeat. Dover
College, Haileybury, Leys School, and Bedford
have been played at different times in the last few
years, but were not encountered in 1895.

The LEYS SCHOOL has always maintained a
high football reputation. Situated on the outskirts

of Cambridge, it has been able to constantly
meet college teams, and so to learn the best football. The Old Leysians, the Old Boys' football
club of the school, has had a great record in
the past. A few years ago it was the premier
London club. The Leys School has never been
of any great size ; the present numbers only
reach 170. Yet their record is a splendid one.
St. Paul's has been played six times ; two matches
were won, three lost, and one drawn. Tonbridge
has been twice defeated, and has won once.
Oundle has been played four times, and beaten
four times. Merchant Taylors' has been beaten
four times, and has won once. Seventeen matches
have been played against Bedford Modern, fifteen
of which have proved wins for the Leys. Mill
Hill has been beaten twice, and has won once.
The school is naturally very keen on the game.
Twice a week is the minimum number of practice
games. On off days the school fifteen practise
passing and kicking. J. C. Isard is the chief
manager of the school games.

In Devonshire there is a knot of schools
amongst which the football rivalry is very keen.
The oldest in foundation, and the largest in

numbers, is Blundell's School. Next comes
Newton College, a school which, under the Rev.
G. T. Warner, a thorough sportsman, and member
of the Rugby Union Committee, rose to 180 boys.
Between Newton and Blundell's the competition
has always been exceedingly keen. Other Rugby
schools are the United Services College, Westward
Ho! and All Hallows' School, Honiton. Of
course I am unable to treat of all the Rugby-
playing schools at any great length. Many I
have not mentioned. There is Dulwich, for
instance, with 610 boys, under Mr. A. H. Gilkes.
Dulwich joined the Union in 1872, and is thus one
of the oldest Union clubs. Amongst the well-
known players that have learnt their football there
are N. F. Henderson, an Oxford International;
W. R. M. Leake, a Cambridge International;
and, of later date, C. M. Wells, whom Mr. R. H.
Cattell in the present book rightly describes as one
of the finest half-backs that England ever produced.
St. Paul's School has over 600 boys on its books.
It was an original member of the Rugby Union, a
representative being present at the meeting which
founded that great society. At Bedford there
are two great football schools, Bedford Grammar

and Bedford Modern, which turn out many fine players. Oundle also follows the Rugby game as does Sherborne, Mill Hill, Epsom, and the Merchant Taylors'. Two of these schools have famous "old boy" clubs in the Old Millhillians and Old Merchant Taylors'. Mill Hill gave the celebrated International, J. H. Dewhurst, to Cambridge. Epsom has been steadily improving, and has now the benefit of Mr. Norman Gardiner's advice in football matters.

CHAPTER XV.

THE NURSERIES OF FOOTBALL IN SCOTLAND.

By C. J. N. Fleming,

Late Captain, Oxford University.

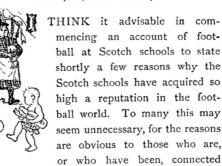 THINK it advisable in commencing an account of football at Scotch schools to state shortly a few reasons why the Scotch schools have acquired so high a reputation in the football world. To many this may seem unnecessary, for the reasons are obvious to those who are, or who have been, connected with them. But to those who know little or nothing about them, a few facts may not be uninteresting.

To begin with, there is a very keen competition

among the schools for the championship, an
honour which, it should be noticed, is its own
reward, for it brings no cup or other tangible
memento to the winner. As a natural consequence of this rivalry, the football played by the
schools reaches a high standard, and for a proof
of this I ask you to look at the performances
of Scottish schoolboys after leaving school. You
will always find the Scotch International fifteen
composed almost entirely of men who learnt
their football at one or other of these great
nurseries of football. Thus of the fifteen which
defeated England at Glasgow, in March, 1896,
Fettes, Merchiston, Loretto, the Edinburgh
Academy, and George Watson's, had each two
representatives, composing in all two-thirds of the
side ; a proportion quite large enough to prove the
excellence of the football played at the schools
from which the players came. With the exception
of Fettes and Loretto, very few of the Scotch
schools send boys on to the Universities ; but
though Fettes and Loretto are not of any great
size, as judged by English standards—for between
them they have only about 350 boys on an average
—yet the success of Fettes and Loretto boys at

the English Universities has been remarkable. In the University match of the season 1888–89, for example, no fewer than ten of the players were from Fettes or Loretto. In the season 1882–83 seven old Lorettonians were included in the famous Oxford team captained by Harry Vassall. For five years—from 1887–88 to 1891–92—the captain of the Cambridge Rugby team was a Scotch schoolboy, three out of the five hailing from Fettes. Lastly, in the Scotch team which so thoroughly beat England at Raeburn Place, in 1894, two of the nine forwards were actually still at school, namely, W. McEwan, of the Edinburgh Academy, and G. Neilson, of Merchiston.

It would be superfluous to add more to show how thoroughly the men must have been taught their football while at school. I will now attempt to point out why it is that these schoolboys reach so high a standard of football excellence, and what it is that develops their keenness for the game.

It is sometimes thought that the boys are older at the Scotch than at the English schools. But this is not the case. It is true, however, that a school team will probably contain two or three boys who will be nineteen before they leave. Yet, at the same time, any one who will take the trouble to inquire will probably be astonished to discover how young some of their best players are. It is no uncommon thing for a boy to get into his school fifteen before he is sixteen years of age, and in another couple of seasons—that is to say, before he is eighteen—he will probably have developed into a big strong lad, and a capital player besides. Again, it is thought that the Scotch boy is naturally bigger and stronger than his English *confrère.* Without admitting that such is invariably the case, it certainly would seem that the majority of Scotch boys develop faster than English, and, as is perhaps of more importance, the Scotch boy is, as a rule, capitally reared. Before he comes to school he will probably have spent a great deal of time in the open air and in manly pursuits, such as fishing, boating, golfing, walking, and in many cases shooting. Of course such a training is the best possible basis for athletic excellence. It may not make the boys very clever, but it gives them a fine physique. Yet, after all, any exceptional advantage that may thus accrue to a Scotch boy is but slight, for many

English boys must be brought up under similar conditions.

What really gives the Scotch schools an advantage over the English is, as I have already stated, the competition for the school championship; and that is only possible through the fortunate accident that practically all the schools are clustered round Edinburgh. It is scarcely necessary to enlarge upon the effects produced by this competition. It is easy to imagine the keenness to represent the school, the trouble taken to get fit, the cheerfulness to train which does not merely affect a few of the bigger fellows at the top, but goes right through the school to the very bottom ; all are possessed of the great truth that if the small boys get slack and do not train, the future school fifteens will suffer. In addition to this, not only do first teams of each school compete, but the second and third as well ; occasionally, I believe, there have been as many as ten fifteens from one school playing ten of another. To get even into a third fifteen a boy will make every effort possible ; while such enthusiasm exists amongst the players, it is scarcely a matter of surprise that the football is of a very high order.

Many people may wonder why Scotch school cricket is not better than it is. There is the same inter-school competition at cricket as at football, but somehow neither the enthusiasm nor the result is the same. The truth is that Rugby football seems to suit the Scotch genius, and cricket does not. Football is, in my opinion, the best game for schools in Scotland, or anywhere else for that matter. It can be learnt after a boy is fourteen or fifteen years of age, while cricket, like golf, should be learnt as young as possible. As an exercise and a safety-valve cricket cannot compare with football in schools. I feel that I am certainly right in saying that the main element in the success of Scotch football is the school competition, although school cricket does not improve in a like manner under like circumstances. Without this competition, it would be like attempting to keep up Oxford rowing without the eights.

Another advantage gained by the fact of the schools being grouped round Edinburgh is that they never want for club matches. Not only on Saturdays will first and second fifteens from each school have matches with clubs, but very often the school fifteen will have a match against a scratch team during the week as well. In this way a school team will play, perhaps, eighteen matches in the season. The advantage gained by playing so often together is obvious. It teaches the boys the correct game, for more is learnt in one match against good players than in weeks of practice alone. Finally, the boys on off days and at odd times see a very fair amount of club football, not to mention the more important matches, such as Trials and Internationals.

When all these things are considered, it is not surprising that the Scotch schools are able to play the Rugby game so well.

Now of the schools themselves, Fettes College, an imposing building just on the north side of Edinburgh, is the leading boarding school. Merchiston, on the south side of Edinburgh, is an older school, though not so large. Loretto is at Musselburgh, seven miles from Edinburgh. There are two great day schools besides—the well-known Edinburgh Academy and George Watson's School. These schools are much larger than the boarding schools I have mentioned, George Watson's having well over a thousand pupils. Besides these schools encircling Edinburgh, there

are two other boarding schools—Blair Lodge, at
Polmont, half-way between Glasgow and Edinburgh ; and Trinity College, Glenalmond, in
Perthshire. The latter, though they enter into
the competition by playing all the schools, have
never yet attained a high place, owing mainly to
their isolated position. I must also mention
Craigmount School, which is now defunct, but
which in its day turned out many famous players,
two of the best known in the South being the
brothers Mason and Martin Scott, of Cambridge ;
while in 1896 two old Craigmount boys played
for Scotland—T. Scott, of Langholm, and J. H.
Cowper, of the West of Scotland.

The inter-school competition has now been going
on for more than twenty years. Football was played
at Merchiston and the Academy in the sixties, and
they were the first to set the example of an annual
match. Loretto, Craigmount, and Fettes joined
in, and by 1875 the school competition was in full
swing. These five schools all play one another
twice a year, once before Christmas, and a return
match afterwards. The struggle to finish the
season as champion school has, from the foundation of the competition, been extraordinarily keen.

In the early days, the Edinburgh Academy had the greatest reputation, but its success gradually departed from it, and after Craigmont had fallen out of the competition early in the eighties, it was left to Fettes, Merchiston, and Loretto, to fight out the battle. Blair Lodge, however, and George Watson's within the last ten years have come to the front. The Edinburgh Academy, too, has regained its prestige, and the championship now lies between Fettes, Merchiston, Loretto, Blair Lodge, George Watson's, and the Edinburgh Academy. The school which suffers the least number of defeats is the victor, though, of course, this sometimes leads to a division of honours. In the season 1894–5, for instance, Fettes, Loretto, and the Academy were reckoned equal, as they had each sustained one defeat. The two matches a season which are arranged between each school cannot always be played, owing to frost, epidemics, or some other reason. But whenever there is a close fight the best of good sportsmanship is always shown ; if a match falls through at the date appointed between two schools, who are running a neck-and-neck race, they invariably manage to bring off the postponed game, and avoid taking any advantage at the hands of fortune.

It would be rather invidious to attempt to classify the schools in order of merit. Indeed, it would be impossible, for they vary from year to year, but Merchiston certainly merits the place of honour, not only for the number of times they have been champions, but for the high standard of football which, despite their small numbers, they have invariably maintained from the very start until now.

I should not feel that I had completed this sketch of the Scotch schools without giving a few details of the method they pursue in the organization of the games, and pointing out what we may learn from their management. The system followed at all the schools is practically the same, though, of course, each school differs in its minor arrangements—differences which usually are due to variations in the hours of school or want of space in the playing fields. In the following remarks I will therefore speak more especially of the system pursued at Fettes, with which I happen to be familiar, though, as I said before, it does not essentially differ from that which is followed elsewhere.

The fundamental principle, which is the basis of all the athletic training, is that every boy, unless prevented by illness or other good cause, must once a day at least change into flannels and take exercise. After football has commenced, which it usually does about the beginning of October, the boys play that game three days a week, and on the other days go for runs. These runs are fixed "grinds," of the average length of two and a half to three miles. As alternatives to these runs, they may play fives, or games at hockey, or Association football. Frequently they are sent to the field to punt about, or practise kicking before they go their run. In addition to this every boy has two classes a week in the gymnasium, in which he goes through Swedish drill and gymnastics; the swimming bath is open every afternoon. Voluntary gymnastics are also popular, both in the gymnasium in the afternoon, and, more especially, in the dormitories at night, where dumb-bells and Indian clubs are in constant use. In this manner every boy in the school gets through a considerable amount of physical exercise, both in the open air and within doors—a good all-round training not devoted to one particular set of muscles.

S

Football is played by games in which the boys are arranged according to size and merit. Care is taken not to let big hulking boys, who are not much good, play in a small game, where they would be able to bully or damage the others. For these games to be successful, it is absolutely necessary that they should be supervised. This is generally done by the bigger boys, who will referee for part of the game, and get relieved for the other part. The fact that a good player is refereeing will keep the game keen and up to the mark. Further, the referee sees that the rules are enforced, for it is wonderful what rules small boys play when left to themselves. He also is able to do a great deal of coaching. There is one school where the bigger boys, so 'tis said, are armed with sticks, and if they find any loafer in a lower game, they apply that stick in a merciless manner. Though such Spartan methods are somewhat extreme, it is all important that the lower games should be kept clear of the loafer. It is an excellent practice to recognize and reward merit at once by putting the enthusiastic boy up into a higher game, and putting down any slacker into the place he has vacated.

As most schools will have three teams at least playing on a Saturday, it is not difficult to find out the real worth of a player, nor is it difficult to select a representative fifteen.

The training of a fifteen need not be thought much about. When the boys play in so many matches as they do in the Scotch schools, they do not need systematic training. Two, or at the most three, games a week is amply sufficient to keep them fit, and even at that there is a considerable risk of the boys getting stale. The fifteen, as at Fettes, should go through some gymnastics every day, though they do not absolutely need those forms of exercise. The work should be simple, such as climbing ropes, or the bridge ladder, or easy work on the parallel bars. Once football has fairly started, long runs are not necessary for the team, though if the weather is very wet, they may be substituted for a game. On the days that football is not played, the entire team should practise sprinting, the forwards dribbling and passing while running as fast as they can, the backs both passing and kicking. This sprinting must take place regularly, and there must be no slacking while it is in progress. Very light work should be done the day before a big match. It is, however, quite impossible to state the quantity necessary, for that will depend upon circumstances. Either the captain or some master must take upon himself the duties of trainer, and decide what additional exercise is required, and when the team must take it.

I have but a few more suggestions to make to those, whether masters or boys, who manage the games of a school. There must be regular coaching, not only of the team, but of the younger boys as well. The games must be organized and carefully looked after, and young players who show any promise must be at once taken in hand, encouraged, and coached. It would, perhaps, be not uninteresting to add the characteristics of a young boy, who may develop into a good player. A boy of twelve to fourteen, who is fat, clumsy perhaps, but big jointed, with big feet and hands, should at once be marked. He will probably develop into a big fellow, and should make a forward. Yet while he is young, he will probably show up badly beside a smart little fellow who has been set up by a too early training. You want for a football player a good rough colt, not a

THE DISADVANTAGE OF HURRY—"NO CHARGE"

dapper little park hack. The characteristics are wide hips, broad shoulders, and plenty of flesh in a young boy. Of course there is another type of build—lithe and wiry. This in a young boy will probably appear as loosely jointed, tall, and thin, and will be remarkable for quickness and activity —a very useful type for either a forward or a back ; but it is a type that wants strength, and until it gets strength it will not be of much value in a school team. Strength often does not come until development has stopped, which is too late for a schoolboy player. Thus I should advise you, as a general rule, to keep an eye on the stout, fleshy type.

As for moral qualities, of course, pluck, intelligence, and plenty of resource are required ; but these are as nothing, strange as it may seem, when compared to bad temper. By bad temper I do not mean a form of obstinate sulkiness, which is the mark of weakness, but the passion which bursts forth into uncontrollable fits of rage. This is a quality which most people check in a young boy, as perhaps it is necessary that it should be checked. Yet, as a matter of fact, it is the one great quality which will make a football player. A boy who possesses such a temper will soon learn to control it, and it is that which will drive him to play with dash and energy. Indeed, football is the salvation of such a character. This mass of latent energy, which might otherwise form a somewhat dangerous ingredient in a man's character, finds in football an excellent safety-valve.

Before closing this article on Scotch school football, I feel it a duty to mention the name of Dr. H. H. Almond, the head-master of Loretto, for it is to him more than to any other that the success which the Scotch schools have attained in athletics is due. His influence for good on the Scotch schools has been enormous, and I believe it has not by any means been confined to the Scotch schools. When the spirit of athleticism was but weak and young, he fostered it, reared it, and fought for it. For many years he has held before us the ideal of manly pluck and physical vigour, which is the crown of athleticism. He has shown us how necessary are such games as Rugby football if we are to lead a healthy life in this age of refined civilization. It is the earnest wish of all who know him that Dr. Almond may long be spared to carry on his good work at Loretto.

I append the results of the Scotch Football Championship since its institution.

1880-1.	Merchiston.	1889-90.	Fettes.
1881-2.	Loretto.	1890-1.	Merchiston.
1882-3.	Merchiston.	1891-2.	Loretto.
1883-4.	Merchiston.	1892-3.	Blair Lodge.
1884-5.	Fettes.	1893-4.	Blair Lodge.
1885-6.	Fettes.	1894-5.	No championship owing to the number of matches abandoned on account of the frost.
1886-7.	Fettes Merchiston equal.		
1887-8.	Merchiston.		
1888-9.	Merchiston.	1895-6.	Merchiston.

CHAPTER XVI.

THE FOOTBALL SUITABLE FOR SCHOOLS—A VOICE FROM SCOTLAND.

By H. B. Tristram,
Oxford University and English International, 1883-4-5.

"IF it were not for football,
I wouldn't be a school-
master." So writes a
modern head - master ;
and any one who knows
anything about schools
recognizes the fact that football is one of the most
valuable institutions we have.
It is a mere truism to say
that boys ought to have regular daily exercise.
They have an exuberance of animal spirits,

which they must work off somehow. If the
ordinary system of a school does not provide a
sensible and satisfactory way of doing this, boys
will find out a way for themselves, foolish probably,
and certainly unsatisfactory. Of course they can
hardly play football six days in the week, especially
if they play the game as it ought to be played.
But football is an admirable nucleus, round which
all sorts of other games may cluster. It is easy
to write any number of platitudes about its advantages in schools — how it encourages pluck,
endurance, and the like ; how it improves the
physique, and strengthens the constitution ; how,
even if it does occasionally give the surgeon some
work to do, it takes away a great deal more from
the physician ; how it develops a readiness of
resource, and a quickness in seeing and grasping
opportunities. All this is undoubtedly true, and
of great importance ; but the value of football
rests almost more on the fact that it is such an
excellent safety valve. Cricket in its season is a
poor substitute, and I know of nothing else that
fulfils all the requirements of a good school game
so well as football.

Of course there are a certain number of boys

who are physically unable to play; and for this
unfortunate class the schools must do the best
they can. People who do not sympathize with
the game will continue to harangue against its
brutality and roughness; but it is the duty
of schoolmasters to see that it is not brutal,
and that the robustness, which is one of its
greatest charms, never degenerates into coarse-
ness. If football is to be compulsory in schools,
parents have the right to demand that there
shall be no unnecessary danger. But really the
danger is much exaggerated. Boys with supple
joints and muscles are far less liable to sprains
and breaks than firmly-set men. It is, perhaps,
against injuries to the head that we have to
guard most carefully. They are the most dangerous and the most subtle, and their effects last
the longest.

Now, in this respect—though I am inclined to
think in this respect only—Association football has
an advantage over Rugby as the chief game of a
school; though I must confess I have had no experience of the working of Association as such.
Accidents to the head are almost unknown under
Association rules; but, unfortunately, it is not so

in Rugby. Whereas a broken leg will probably be all right again in a couple of months, a boy may feel the effects of concussion of the brain for years. Nevertheless, Rugby is a better form of physical training than Association. It exercises the upper limbs far more. Following the remarkable statistics of chest measurements at Merchiston, which has certainly produced some of the best scrummagers in Scotland, we find that since that school has to a certain extent given up the old style of tight scrummaging, the average chest girth of the boys has most distinctly gone down.

Further, the practical consideration of space and numbers makes Rugby more convenient for schools. In a school of two hundred it is very much easier to find room for six games of thirty a side than for eight or nine games of twenty-two a' side. And though, perhaps, a Rugby full back may not get very much exercise, he always gets a good deal more than an Association goal-keeper.

But whatever kind of football is played, there are two points which ought to be impressed on every boy as soon as he begins to learn the game.

The first is to keep his temper. And that for a boy is often an uncommonly hard thing to do. Boys are very quick to resent anything that seems like unfair treatment. Say that a player tackles with unnecessary vigour when the runner is already held. Some one retaliates, and very soon the gulf which exists between hard play and rough play is bridged over. In Rugby football weight and strength confer advantages enough on their possessor without being used to knock an opponent out of time by hurling him against the boundary palings.

The second is to accept the referee's decision without a grumble. Referees make mistakes, and a good one is generally the first to admit the fact. If a boy is too fond of finding fault with the decisions, it is not a bad plan to get him to take charge of the whistle for a day ; and after one experience of a scrambling game, he will probably be more lenient in the future.

But it is quite hopeless to expect football to be of real use in schools unless boys are keen on it. To make boys keen on it, there must, in the first place, be plenty of matches. In this the Scottish schools are exceptionally fortunate. They can

get matches regularly every week, not only for
their first, but also for their second and third
fifteens ; besides occasional matches for still lower
teams. Some of the Edinburgh schools play each
other with nine fifteens on the same day. These
frequent foreign matches, combined with the
intense rivalry between the schools, maintain
the interest in football ; and the competition
for places in any team, especially if the team
be a successful one, is naturally very keen. But
sometimes, if the season is a long one, and
the fifteen has a run of bad fortune, there is
a danger of football beginning to drag. The
games get slack, the play gets worse, and the
school suffers in more ways than in its football.
If keenness is to be kept up in a bad year, the
game must have an interest of its own, apart from
the extra excitement of matches. It must be
remembered that many boys turn out on the
football field, not because they like the game,
but because they are obliged to play. And so,
if football is to fulfil its mission, it must be
made as interesting as possible for the ordinary
player.

A good deal of the modern legislation seems

designed to attract spectators. But the schools are entirely independent of spectators, and ought not to be influenced in the least by such an element. Their duty is to maintain the interest of the players. Now I am not by any means prepared to say that the old-fashioned tight scrummaging was more interesting to the boy-player than the fast modern game. That it was a better physical training for boys I am sure ; and the Merchiston statistics, to which I have already referred, go a long way to prove the use of scrummaging. But of this I am certain that the game at present played by the best clubs in England and Wales is not adapted for boys. It is too fast, and puts too great a premium on mere pace. In the first place, it is a heavy strain on growing boys, and makes it impossible for them to play as often as they used to do in days gone by. Secondly, the inferior and slower players on a side get disgusted with futile efforts to overtake an opponent, who, as wearisome experience has already taught them, is far too speedy for them. It is no wonder that mediocre forwards do not care for a game in which they have only got to shove hard till one side or the other has heeled out, and then limber up,

and trot quietly off to the scene of the next
scrummage.

Scotland has not yet fallen in love with four
three-quarters. She still puts her chief trust in
her formidable forwards. And it is the same, for
the most part, among the schools. Year after
year Merchiston sacrifices everything for the forwards; and though in numbers all the leading
schools, save Loretto, have been larger, Merchiston
has been beaten fewer times than any other
of them. Those who have played against Merchiston teams know that their victories are entirely
due to their forwards. It is worth noting that
while that school has furnished a great many
forwards to the Scotch teams, it has turned out
comparatively few backs. I believe it is a very
difficult thing for a school to produce good
scrummagers and good backs at the same time.
If the forwards are to be exceptionally brilliant,
the backs must be to a certain extent sacrificed ;
while if the backs are to become expert, the
forwards must play to them. Scotland, with her
limited number of clubs from which to draw, is in
rather the same position. But Scotland has of
late years been exceptionally lucky in being able

to get her forwards from Scotland, and her backs very much from England, where they have a better chance of obtaining opportunities of learning the meaning of combination.

Now I have been told by boys who have gone up from Scotch schools to the English Universities, or who have joined clubs in the South of England, that the forward game played there seems dull and uninteresting compared with the game they were accustomed to play at school. If a respectable, average forward considers the game dull, what are we to expect from the inferior players ? And the forwards are the people whose interests we have got chiefly to consider. They form the great majority of the players ; and, besides, backs will always have plenty of work—and interesting work —to get through, whatever the style of play; though they may find it more difficult to make chances for themselves, and will certainly not have the same number of easy chances made for them, as they have when all the forwards are locked in the scrummage.

As I have already said, I do not think the four three-quarter game is suited for schools, though, if you get the right men, it will undoubtedly

A FORWARD RUSH

win matches. But the winning of matches is not the primary object of football in schools. We want a game that is interesting for all the players, and at the same time is a sound physical training.

The abolition of heeling out—horribly reactionary though it may sound—would, I believe, do a great deal towards this. Of course, under the old rules all the forwards on the heeling-out side were off-side as soon as the ball was played by the half-back behind them, and so they had no right to be in the way of their opponents.

The Americans soon understood this, and eventually found it necessary to legalize interference which they could not easily prevent. As soon as the off-side rule was abrogated the complicated "wedge" and "tandem" formations of American football came into existence. This "tandem" play is not entirely unknown with us. I have seen a half-back with the ball run round the back of the scrummage, and be so covered by his companion on the other side, that neither the half-back on that side nor the nearest three-quarter could get at him ; and yet it would have been hard for a referee to say that he was

T

more guilty than any of his forwards who had "heeled out" to him.

I am conservative enough to think that the first great mistake of the new legislation was the legalization of off-side play in the scrummage ; and the second, the penalizing of the natural antidote, the half-backs coming round to their opponents' side of the scrummage. According to the old and excellent rules of off-side, as long as the opponents were playing the ball, a player could never be off-side, and could stand and play where he liked.

I am sure that if we could here retrace our steps a little, we should make a better game of it for schools. And in this I have the support of Mr. Burgess, who has been most closely identified with Scotch school football for the last sixteen years, and who is undoubtedly the best coach of forwards in Scotland. It would not be a return to the long and tight scrummaging—though I fancy Mr. Burgess would be glad enough if it were, for he is a firm believer in the value of the scrummage in the physical training of boys. We can get plenty of forward play without that. There will be more foot-work and more dribbling among the forwards, and they will begin to regard themselves as something more than a screen behind which their backs can develop the attack. Those who remember a somewhat famous match between a strong team of the Edinburgh Academicals and Loretto, in 1881, will be ready to admit that the art of taking the ball away at the side of the scrummage, either by screwing it or by merely sliding off the opponents, was not unknown even in those dark ages. The feat was more difficult then, for no one was allowed to get in front of the ball in the scrummage, and so the ball had to be kept in the front row, and not stowed away at the back as it is now.

One other point there is, which would improve the school game—for forwards certainly, and probably for backs also. Banish the practice of falling on the ball. I believe it to be dangerous. And the chief reason why more accidents have not resulted from it is that players are chivalrous enough to dislike the idea of risking kicking a man lying on the ground. At the same time, it is for this same reason that it is so successful. If dribbling forwards did kick hard at the ball when an opponent was falling on it, I believe

they would sometimes be able to get it away,
but there would very often be a serious accident.
A method of play which depends for its success
on an appeal *ad misericordiam* can hardly be
considered in accord with the spirit of football.
The practice, I fancy, only dates from about 1882
or 1883, and was probably introduced to meet
the growing tendency towards shorter scrummages
and more dribbling. But this is the sort of game
that we want at school ; for my experience leads
me to the conclusion that it is the game which
boy-forwards will like best ; and that, I maintain,
is one of the two great objects we ought to have
in view.

In conclusion, whatever may be the style of
play in a school, there are always sure to be a
certain number of boys, especially on the lower
sides, who do not like the game, and will only
play it under compulsion. A few of these, from
a sense of duty, may play up fairly hard, but the
majority will not, unless the game is absolutely
compulsory. It may sound rather brutal, but
these boys never will like the game until they do
play up ; and so the only thing to be done is to
have some one there who will not only show

them how to play, but will also make them play. There are lots of boys who used to hate football when they always slacked, but found out, when they began to play hard, that it was not such a bad game, after all.

CHAPTER XVII.

RUGBY FOOTBALL ABROAD.

PERHAPS no evidence can be adduced that will more surely prove the intrinsic worth of the Rugby Union game than its growing popularity abroad. The majority of players are, it is true, of English blood. Despite of difficulties of climate and dangers of fever, wherever our race penetrates the goal-posts spring up like the mango tree under the hands of an Indian conjurer. In our colonies the interest taken in football has been fostered by a series of tours. English teams of no little repute have travelled to Australia, New Zealand, and the Cape, and shown to the colonists the latest developments of the game as it is played in the great football centres at home. Undismayed by their defeats, our kinsmen across the seas have remodelled their antiquated style of play on the lines suggested by the good football

shown to them. Every year they advance in
skill, while their enthusiasm remains unabated.
In China, in India, in Buenos Ayres, scattered
clubs prove that whether the members be hardy
"tykes" or canny Scots, dashing Irishmen or
tricky Welshmen, they are one in remembering
the game they have learnt to love at home.

But Rugby football is finding devotees amongst
other nationalities besides our own. The keenness
for athleticism which changed the social life of
England in the sixties is now steadily growing
in France and Germany. It is eagerly fostered
by the authorities, who rejoice in national amusements which tend to improve rather than weaken
the physique of the army. Already our supremacy
is threatened in rowing, in cycling, and in running ;
in a few years we possibly may find ourselves
struggling to maintain our premier position in
the football field. Shall we ever be forced to take
a secondary place amongst the athletic nations of
the world ? "No ; the idea is ridiculous," nine
out of ten Englishmen would answer. But is it
so ridiculous ? Military training is of immense
advantage in developing the national thews and
sinews ; in one sense it broadens the national

chest, though, as political economists tell us, it
reduces it in another.   As our towns grow bigger—
and they are vast enough as it is—more children
will be bred in them, to the great disadvantage
of the poor little weaklings.   Childhood will pass
into youth, and youth into manhood, in the same
close atmosphere.   "But what of our games?"
you ask.   Sad to relate, with the growth of professionalism, there is a noticeable tendency amongst
the working classes to prefer watching the matches
to playing in them.   They like to assemble in
masses to do a bit of betting, and cheer their
favourite team to victory on a Saturday; but exercise for thirty men is a poor return for the idleness
of thirty thousand.   Here foreigners will hold us
at a disadvantage.   The much-despised military
system, which we are never tired of pointing at and
jeering at, while thanking our stars that it does
not exist in England, pulls this mass of humanity
out of the narrow streets.   It drills them and
punches them in the back till they stand up
straight, and shows them how to square their
shoulders and step out from the hips; it feeds them
on healthy food and gives them good clothing;
it lodges them in spotlessly clean and perfectly

sanitary barracks ; it teaches them discipline—a
most necessary quality nowadays, for it is still
true that no man can command who cannot obey ;—
in short, it turns them into respectable members
of the human family. However, this chapter is
on football abroad, and to that let us return with
what speed we may.

America numbers almost as many enthusiastic
supporters of football as we do ourselves. Their
national game, however, differs considerably from
ours. " An improvement," they term it, but
Englishmen can hardly be expected to coincide
with their view of the question. Probably the
foundation was the Rugby Union game, and
the "improvements" are the work of American
ingenuity. In some of the Western districts
Rugby football is played. But with these exceptions the American game is universal. Without
entering into details, it will be enough to say
that the chief object of the players is the protection of the man who runs with the ball. There
is no off-side rule, and the forwards form a line
or a wedge in front of him, and charge down the
field. The tackling is of the hardest. That " all
is fair in love, war, and American football," might

have been a revised version of the old proverb
a few years ago. Although since then there has
been a change for better, the great Inter-University
matches are fought out with a terrible determination. The "butcher's bill" is a long one; and,
unlike our English game, substitutes are held in
waiting to take the place of the injured players.
The enthusiasm is immense; it is not too much
to say that on the day of the Yale *v.* Princeton
match all New York is worked up to a pitch of
extraordinary excitement. Horns blow and flags
wave; carriages clatter through the streets carrying
cheering loads of the college "boys"; all the hotels
and half the houses are draped with the colours
of the contesting Universities; and the vast throng
which gathers to see the game numbers amongst
it the smartest members of New York society.

The training of the teams is very severe. For
some months all their meals are taken at a common training table, and the food is supplied from
the funds of the club. The "expenses" of an
American football team would indeed make an
English amateur stare. To learn the game is no
easy matter. A code of signals is established.
On the captain shouting a prearranged number,

the field changes like a kaleidoscope. The
moment he hears it, each player knows what is
expected of him, and in what direction he has to
run. It is easy to imagine that such a perfection
of drill is not quickly acquired. During the day,
when no match is being played, the team practises
in an enclosed ground. Great care is taken that
no member of the enemy's forces shall spy out the
formations under rehearsal. An amusing story is
told of a certain University team that had been
practising for many weeks a system, never previously attempted, which they felt convinced would
astonish and puzzle their opponents in the great
match of the season. However, a week before the
date fixed for that important event a casual undergraduate, while inspecting a neighbouring water-
tower, was horrified to discover two of the foe
concealed near the top, armed with field-glasses
and note-books. They were quickly routed out ;
but the chance of springing a surprise on their
foes was lost to the home team. The tribula-
tion that ensued can better be imagined than
described.

The members of the University football teams
are most important personages. They can easily

be distinguished in private life by their long hair
and their self-conscious bearing. *À propos* of
this, I once heard of an incident worth relating
which occurred to a friend in an American hotel.
It was in New York, and the hotel was among
the largest and most splendidly appointed of them
all. My friend was lounging in the hall, when
a quiet little man came in and sat down in a
corner. There was some watching and whispering amongst the Americans present. He looked
round to discover what was the cause of the com-
motion, and, seeing his curiosity, a tall, thin man
arose from a neighbouring chair, and, stalking
solemnly up to him, remarked, "I reckon, sir, that
you aire a stranger?" He admitted the fact.
"Then you do not know who that is, perhaps?"
No—my friend did not. The Yank looked grieved.
"That man, sir," he said slowly, "can write a
cheque for ten million dollars!" Without waiting
for the diverse expressions of surprise with which
he was evidently convinced his communication
would be received, he retired to his seat. The
excitement soon subsided; then suddenly a door
was flung open, and in walked a vast speci-
men of humanity, with a mass of hair over his

eyes that would not have disgraced a buffalo. He
seized a chair with one hand, banged it down, and
called loudly and somewhat profanely to a waiter
for liquid refreshment. The wave of excitement
that went round the circle was almost tidal in its
intensity. Again my friend stared in astonish-
ment, and again turned only to discover the tall,
thin man at his elbow. " I reckon you know who
that is, anyhow," he said in a confident voice.
" Wall, darn it," he exclaimed as he received an
answer in the negative, " where do you come from ?
Don't know him ? Why, sir, he is the CAPTAIN
OF THE —— UNIVERSITY FOOTBALL TEAM ! "
And with a sigh of regret that such ignorance
was possible, he left my friend to meditate on the
fallacy of the statement that great wealth is the
only distinction in Yankeeland.

At the time of the World's Fair at Chicago,
Yale challenged Oxford University to a football
match. It was to be played at Chicago, and
expenses would be guaranteed. Of course the
scheme was impossible. As a writer of the day
expressed it, " Will this mean that eleven Yanks
are to play fifteen Englishmen at Rugger, or that
eleven Englishmen are to play fifteen Yanks at

Chicagger ?—if I may use the term." After some negotiations, the offer was withdrawn.

In Canada the game is in a flourishing condition. Amongst the roll of unions and clubs which are members of the English Rugby Union are the Ontario Rugby Union, with its centre at Toronto, and the Canadian Rugby Union, with its centre at Montreal. Ontario has a regular system of senior and junior competitions. The colleges of Toronto and Ottawa turn out excellent teams, and the Toronto football ground is amongst the finest in the world.

In Australia and New Zealand football has long been in existence. In some parts of Australia, especially in Victoria, there is a nondescript game, which is a sort of mixture of Rugby and Association, but in general the Rugby game is played. In New Zealand the Rugby game holds undisputed sway. The number of New Zealand clubs and unions that are members of the English Rugby Union is remarkable. Amongst them are the Auckland Union, the Canterbury Club, the Dunedin Club, the Otago Union, the Wellington Club, and the Wellington Union. In 1888 Shaw and Shrewsbury took out an English fifteen to play matches in the two colonies. A strong team was got together, although the Rugby Union Committee did not feel justified in extending its patronage and support to the tour. Some thirty-five matches were arranged under Rugby rules; of these the visitors won twenty-seven. While in Australia, they foolishly, as many people thought, agreed to play under the Victorian code, of which they were entirely ignorant. Under these rules they played eighteen matches, of which eleven were lost, one drawn, and six won. They were splendidly received, and certainly had a most enjoyable time. That they improved colonial football is an undoubted fact. During their stay in New Zealand, the islanders made such progress in the art of passing, that they had considerable difficulty in winning return matches with clubs which they had at first easily defeated.

Before this English team returned home, a team of New Zealanders arrived in England. Their visit was well timed, for the International matches were disorganized by a quarrel between England and the other Unions. They were of mixed race, consisting of English colonists, half-breeds, and Maoris. The "New Zealand Native Football

Representatives" they termed themselves, but as the "Maoris" they were invariably known. At first crowds flocked to their matches, as to some entertainment after the fashion of the "Swazi village;" afterwards they went to see good football played. The Maoris discarded the native head-dresses and mats in which they appeared on the football field after their arrival, as soon as their real merit was recognized. In passing they were at first very weak though they steadily improved; but scrummaging was always their strong point. This is hardly to be wondered at, considering that three of their team weighed over fourteen stone, while five more were thirteen stone and more. In twenty-five weeks they played no less than seventy-four matches, of which they won forty-nine, drew five, and lost twenty. The worst features of the tour were a tendency they displayed towards unnecessary roughness and an objectionable habit they never quite discarded of disputing the decisions of the referee. Indeed, on one memorable occasion, when they were playing England, they left the field in a body as a protest at a decision by Mr. Rowland Hill, who was the referee. For this they were deservedly called upon to apologize before the tour was allowed to proceed. The writer remembers "spectating" at a match between the Maoris and Devonshire. One of the Devon forwards came off the field sorrowfully rubbing his leg. "What is the matter?" I asked. "Why," he said, "I came to play football, not to join in a dog fight! One of the beggars has bitten me in the calf!"

At the Cape—that fortunate colony which is at present supplying three-fourths of the foreign news in the London papers—football is immensely popular. Both Rugby and Association football is played, but the former has by far the greater number of adherents. At one time a mongrel game compiled from the rules of both these forms of football seemed to be gaining ground, but it has now practically disappeared. In 1891, a team under the patronage of the Rugby Union, and with expenses guaranteed by Mr. Cecil Rhodes, sailed for the Cape. The tour was a great success, nineteen matches being played, all of which were won—an unrivalled performance in the history of football tours. The grounds, however, were and are much against enjoyable games. The sun scorches the grass until the field of play

U

is practically composed of gravel, dust, sand and small stones. This year a team has repeated the experiment of 1888. They are fairly strong, the Irish forward contingent containing some brilliant players. The Colonials have considerably improved in passing and the screwing tactics of forward play ; but although several matches have been drawn, none—at the time at which I write— have been lost by our representatives.

In Europe the game is making slow but steady progress. It was an uphill struggle at first. Rugby football presented few attractions to a paternal police, unused to consider athletics in the light of a national benefit. In France and Belgium the game was frequently stopped by the gendarmes in its early days. But all this has been changed, and there are now several clubs in Paris that are under the special patronage of the President. Their enthusiasm is great, and through the frequent visits of English teams their play steadily improves. I was an interested spectator at several of the earlier of these matches, which, in the strictest sense of the word, may be described as International. The play of the French team was, I am forced to admit, rather of a humorous than of a skilful character. The shouts and cries with which they encouraged each other; the wild rejoicings, the black despair; the suspicion of perfidy aroused by the conduct of the referee; the embracings on securing an advantage; the hand clapping which answered the British cheers at the conclusion of the game;—all were sufficiently ludicrous, but appeared even more so by comparison with the stolid, business-like demeanour of their opponents. Still, from first to last they invariably played a hard, plucky game, and I have little doubt that in time they will turn out formidable teams that will be "worthy of the steel" of the best clubs amongst us.

In Germany the game has at present taken no great hold. Round the Universities, however, and near places where Englishmen congregate, the goal-posts are to be seen. Occasionally a few Germans join in the games. Newnheim College, which is close to Heidelberg, but which is chiefly frequented by Englishmen and Americans, is the only club in Germany which is a member of the Rugby Union.

Thus has the great game, which sprung from the English school, spread over the world. How far it will extend, and how far it will maintain its popularity, is " in the lap of the gods." All that we who love the game can do is to strive to maintain its high traditions at home, and wish it good speed on its way abroad.

MR. G. ROWLAND HILL.

APPENDIX.

BYE-LAWS OF THE RUGBY FOOTBALL UNION, ETC.,

As passed at the General Meeting held on September 20, 1893, and Amended, 1894-5-6.

1.—The name of the society shall be "THE RUGBY FOOT-BALL UNION," and only clubs entirely composed of amateurs shall be eligible for membership; and its head-quarters shall be in London, where all general meetings shall be held.

2.—The committee, who shall be elected annually, shall consist of the five following officers, namely,—a president, two vice-presidents, an hon. secretary, and an hon. treasurer, and sixteen other members. All past presidents of the Union, who shall have attended two regularly convened committee meetings during the previous year, shall be members of the committee. Seven shall form a quorum; the chairman shall have a casting vote in addition to his first vote. No past president shall be entitled to vote on the selection of teams unless he has been chosen to act on the sub-committee elected for that purpose. Any vacancy in the committee occurring during the year shall be filled up by the committee.

3.—All clubs being members of the Rugby Union in the following districts shall have the following representation on the committee, and may elect the number of representatives on the committee respectively placed opposite their names, namely :—

Cambridge University	One
Cheshire	One
Cumberland and Westmoreland	One
Durham	One
Lancashire	Three
London District	Four
Midland Counties	One
Northumberland	One
Oxford University	One
South-Western District	Two
Yorkshire	Four

Twenty.

The South-Western district shall comprise the counties of Cornwall, Devon, Gloucester, and Somerset, and the London district all clubs and counties not included in any of the above.

All such elections shall be in the hands of the hon. secretary by August 7 ; if not, the new committee shall fill up any vacancies.

The manner in which the above twenty seats are distributed may be altered at any annual general meeting, on the vote of the majority of those present, provided notice of such proposed alteration be given to the hon. secretary not later than August 7.

4.—There shall be sent to each club, not later than August 14 in each year, a list of the twenty representatives so elected, together with the committee's nominations of officers for the ensuing year, namely, a president and two vice-presidents, nominated from the above twenty representatives ; an hon. secretary, not necessarily from the above twenty ; and an hon. treasurer, nominated either from the above twenty, or from the past presidents. Any club has the right to make further nomination of officers only, but any for president or vice-president must be from the twenty elected representatives, for treasurer from the above twenty or from past presidents ; any such nominations must reach the hon. secretary by August 21, and a complete list of all nominations must be sent to each club with the circular calling the annual general meeting.

5.—The election of officers shall take place at each annual general meeting, and shall be decided by a majority of those voting. In case the hon. secretary be elected from the twenty elected representatives, then such representation shall become void, and the county, university, or district shall elect another representative to fill such vacancy. In case a district has to make another election, such must be done within fourteen days of the annual general meeting ; if not so made, the Committee shall fill the vacancy.

6.—Any club willing to conform to the Rules of the Union shall be eligible for membership, but before being admitted, such club must be duly proposed and seconded by two clubs belonging to the Union.

7.—That the annual subscription, payable in advance, of each club belonging to the Union, be £1 1s., with an entrance fee of 10s. 6d., payable on admission. The annual subscriptions of all clubs shall fall due in September. Any club whose subscription has not been paid before March 1 shall be struck off the Union list.

8.—The annual general meeting shall be held in September in each year for the election of officers, the consideration of the bye-laws, laws of the game, and rules as to professionalism, and other business.

9.—Each club shall be entitled to send one representative only to any annual or special general meeting, exclusive of the officers and committee of the Union.

10.—The hon. secretary shall convene a special general

meeting at any time on receiving a requisition to that effect signed by the secretaries of not less than forty clubs belonging to the Union, and stating specific notice of motion.

In case of a special general meeting, such must be held within one month of receipt of requisition, preliminary notice must be sent out by the hon. secretary within ten days of such requisition, and notices of amendment must be received by him within seventeen days of receipt of requisition.

11.—That no bye-law, law of the game, or rule as to professionalism shall be altered, rescinded, or added to, without the consent of at least two-thirds of those present at a general meeting.

12.—Each club shall be furnished with a copy of the bye-laws, laws of the game, and rules as to professionalism, and be bound thereby. In case of infringement thereof by any club or player, such club or player may be punished or expelled by the committee, subject to appeal to a general meeting, except on a matter of fact, when there shall not be any right of appeal.

13.—Notice of any amendment or alteration in the bye-laws, laws of the game, or rules as to professionalism, together with the names of the proposing and seconding clubs, shall be given in writing to the hon. secretary, not later than August 7, a copy of such notice shall be sent to each club not later than August 14 ; and notice of any amendment to such amendment or alteration must be in writing signed by an official of the club making it, and must reach the hon. secretary by August 21, after which each club shall be advised by circular of the date of the annual general meeting, and of all proposed alterations and amendments.

14.—The committee shall have sole control of the funds of the Union. The accounts shall be audited by two auditors, appointed at the previous annual general meeting.

A printed copy of the signed balance-sheet shall be sent to each club, along with the notice calling the annual general meeting.

15.—The committee may at any time before the end of July alter the distribution of the twenty seats ; in case such re-distribution be challenged by any county, university, or district, the next annual general meeting shall be asked to confirm or reject such alteration on the vote of a majority.

16.—The committee shall appoint three trustees, in whose names they may from time to time invest any funds of the Union ; which investment shall be held by the said trustees solely for the furtherance of amateur Rugby football.

17.—Any league or combination of clubs shall be under the authority of and shall obtain the consent of the Union to its formation, and shall be required to submit its proposed rules, and any subsequent alterations thereof, for approval to the Rugby Union committee, who shall have power—

(*a*) To forbid the formation or continuance of such league or combination of clubs in their absolute discretion.

(*b*) To discharge from membership or suspend any club contravening this bye-law.

(*c*) To suspend any club which shall play a match with a club which has been suspended or discharged from membership under the bye-law, or with any club which has been formed out of the nucleus of any suspended club.

18.—In case any difference of opinion arises as to the meaning of any of these bye-laws, such meaning shall be decided by the committee, or, if it occurs at a general meeting, by the chairman thereof ; any such decision shall be recorded in the minutes, and shall be accepted as the true meaning of the bye-law until otherwise interpreted at a general meeting, after due notice has been given.

PLAN OF THE FIELD.

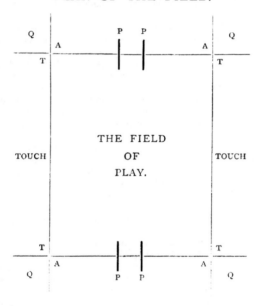

AA, AA.—Goal-lines.   TT, TT. —Touch-lines.
PP, PP.—Goal-posts.   QQ, QQ.—Touch in Goal.

The touch-lines and goal-lines should be cut out of the turf, or otherwise well defined.

The field of play should not exceed 110 yards in length, nor 75 yards in breadth, and should be as near those dimensions as practicable.

The maximum extent of the dead-ball line is 25 yards.

The posts and flags marking the centre and 25 yards lines should be kept well back from the touch-lines.

LAWS OF THE GAME OF FOOTBALL,

AS PLAYED BY

THE RUGBY FOOTBALL UNION.

I.—INTRODUCTION.

1.—The Rugby Game of Football should be played by fifteen players on each side. (Any one coming under the laws of professionalism shall not be allowed to take part in any game under this Union's jurisdiction.) The field of play shall not exceed 110 yards in length, nor 75 in breadth, and shall be as near these dimensions as practicable. The lines defining the boundary of the field of play shall be suitably marked, and shall be called the goal-lines at the ends and the touch-lines at the sides. On each goal-line and equidistant from the touch-lines shall be two upright posts, called goal-posts, exceeding 11 ft. in height, and placed 18 ft. 6 in. apart, and joined by a cross-bar 10 ft. from the ground ; and the object of the game shall be to kick the ball over this cross-bar and between the posts. The game shall be played with an oval ball of as nearly as possible the following size and weight, namely—

Length	...	...	...	...	11 to $11\frac{1}{4}$ in.
Length circumference		...	··	30 „ 31 „
Width circumference		...	...	$25\frac{1}{2}$ „ 26 „
Weight	...	...	...	...	13 „ $14\frac{1}{2}$ ozs.

Hand-sewn and not less than eight stitches to the inch.

II.—GLOSSARY—DUTIES OF OFFICIALS— SCORING.

Glossary of Terms.

2.—The following terms occur in the laws, and have the respective meanings attached to each :—

DEAD-BALL LINE.—Not more than 25 yards behind, and equidistant from the respective goal-lines, and parallel thereto, shall be lines, which shall be called the Dead-ball Lines, and if the ball or player holding the ball touch or cross these lines the ball shall be dead and out of play.

IN-GOAL.—Those portions of the ground immediately at the ends of the field of play and between the touch-lines, produced to the dead-ball lines, are called In-goal. The goal-lines are in-goal.

TOUCH.—Those portions of the ground immediately at the sides of the field of play and between the goal-lines, if produced, are called Touch. The touch-lines and all posts and flags marking these lines, or the centre, or 25 yards lines, are in touch.

TOUCH-IN-GOAL.—Those portions of the ground immediately at the four corners of the field of play, and between the goal and touch-lines, if respectively produced, are called Touch-in-Goal. The corner posts and flags are in touch-in-goal.

A DROP-KICK is made by letting the ball fall from the hands, and kicking it the very instant it rises.

A PLACE-KICK is made by kicking the ball after it has been placed on the ground.

A PUNT is made by letting the ball fall from the hands and kicking it before it touches the ground.

A TACKLE is when the holder of the ball is held by one or more players of the opposite side.

A SCRUMMAGE, which can only take place in the field of play, is when the ball is put down between players who have closed round on their respective sides, and who must have both feet on the ground.

A TRY is gained by the player who first puts his hand on the ball on the ground in his opponents' in-goal.

A TOUCH-DOWN is when a player touches down as above in his own in-goal.

A GOAL is obtained by kicking the ball from the field of play, except from a *punt,* from a kick-off, or from a drop-out, direct (*i.e.* without touching the ground or any player of either side) over the opponents' cross-bar, whether it touch such cross-bar or the goal-posts or not.

KNOCKING-ON and THROWING-FORWARD are propelling the ball by the hand or arm in the direction of the opponents' in-goal; a throw out of touch cannot be claimed as a throw-forward.

A FAIR-CATCH is a catch made direct from a kick or knock-on or throw-forward by one of the opposite side; the catcher must immediately claim the same by making a mark with his heel at the spot where he made the catch.

KICK-OFF is a place-kick from the centre of the field-of-play; the opposite side may not stand within ten yards of the ball, nor charge until the ball be kicked, otherwise another kick-off shall be allowed. If the ball pitch in touch, the opposite side may have it kicked off again.

DROP-OUT is a drop-kick from within 25 yards of the kicker's goal-line; within which distance the opposite side may not charge, otherwise another drop-out shall be allowed. If the ball pitch in touch, the opposite side may have it dropped out again.

At kick-off the ball must reach the limit of ten yards, and at drop-out must reach the 25 yards line. If otherwise, the opposite side may have the ball re-kicked, or scrummaged, at the centre or in the middle of the 25 yards line, as the case may be.

OFF-SIDE.—See Laws 7 and 8.

Referee and Touch-judges.

3.—In all matches a Referee and two Touch-judges must be appointed, the former being mutually agreed upon. The Referee must carry a whistle, which he must blow in the following cases :—

Duties of Referee.

(*a*) When a player makes and claims a fair catch.

(*b*) When he notices rough or foul play or misconduct. For the first offence he shall either caution the player or order him off the ground, but for the second offence he must order him off. If ordered off, the player must be reported by him to this Union.

(*c*) When he considers that the continuation of play is dangerous.

(*d*) When the ball has been improperly put into a scrummage.

(*e*) When he wishes to stop the game for any purpose.

(*f*) If the ball or a player running with the ball touch him.

(*g*) At half-time and no-side, he being the sole time-keeper, having sole power to allow extra time for delays, but he shall not whistle for half-time or no-side until the ball be held or out of play.

(*h*) When a player in a scrummage lifts a foot from the ground before the ball has been put fairly into the scrummage.

(*i*) When he notices any irregularity of play whereby the side committing such gain an advantage.

(*j*) When he notices a breach of Laws 5 and 15.

Powers of Referee.

The Referee shall be sole judge in all matters of fact, but as to matters of law there shall be the right of appeal to the Rugby Union.

Duty of Touch-judges.

The touch-judges shall carry flags, and shall each take one side of the ground, outside the field of play, and the duty of each shall be to hold up his flag when and where the ball goes into touch, and also to assist the Referee, if requested by him, at kicks at goal.

Rules.

4.—The captains of the respective sides shall toss up for the choice of in-goal or the kick-off. Each side shall play an equal time from each in-goal, and a match shall be won by a majority of points; if no point be scored, or the number be equal, the match shall be drawn.

Scoring.

The following shall be the mode of scoring :—

A Try	equals 3 points.
A Penalty Goal	,, 3 ,,
A Goal from a Try (in which case the Try shall not count) ...	,, 5 ,,
Any other Goal	,, 4 ,,

Kick-off.

5.—At the time of the kick-off all the kicker's side shall be behind the ball ; if any are in front, the Referee shall blow his whistle and order a scrummage where the kick-off took place. The game shall be re-started by a kick-off—

(a) After a goal, by the side losing such goal, and

(b) After half-time, by the opposite side to that which started the game.

III.—MODE OF PLAY—DEFINITIONS.

Mode of Play.

6.—When once the game is started, the ball may be kicked or picked up and run with by any player who is on-side, at any time ; except that it may not be picked up—

(*a*) In a scrummage.

(*b*) When it has been put down after it has been fairly held.

(*c*) When it is on the ground after a player has been tackled.

It may be passed or knocked from one player to another, provided it be not passed, knocked, or thrown forward. If a player while holding or running with the ball be tackled and the ball fairly held, he MUST at once put it fairly down between him and his opponents' goal-line.

Off-side.

7.—A player is placed off-side if he enters a scrummage from his opponents' side, or if the ball has been kicked, touched, or is being run with by one of his own side behind him. A player can be off-side in his opponents' in-goal, but not in his own, except where one of his side takes a free kick behind his goal-line, in which case all his side must be behind the ball when kicked.

8.—An off-side player is placed on-side—

(*a*) When an opponent has run five yards with the ball.

(*b*) When the ball has been kicked by, or has touched an opponent.

(*c*) When one of his side has run in front of him with the ball.

(*d*) When one of his side has run in front of him, having kicked the ball when behind him.

An off-side player shall not play the ball, nor during the time an opponent has the ball, run, tackle, or actively or

passively obstruct, nor may he approach within ten yards
of any player waiting for the ball. On any breach of this
law, the opposite side shall be awarded, at their option—

    (*e*) A free kick, the place of such breach being taken as
        the mark.

    (*f*) A scrummage at the spot where the ball was last
        played by the offending side before such breach
        occurred.

Except in the case of unintentional off-side, when a scrummage shall be formed where such breach occurred.

Fair Catch.

9.—If a player makes a fair catch he shall be awarded a
free kick, even though the whistle has been blown for a
knock-on, and he himself must either kick or place the ball.

Free Kicks.

10.—All free kicks may be place-kicks, drop-kicks, or
punts, but must be in the direction of the opponents' goal-
line, and across the kicker's goal-line, if kicked from behind
the same. They may be taken at any spot behind the mark
in a line parallel to the touch-lines. If taken by drop or
punt, the catcher must take the kick ; if taken by a place-
kick, the catcher must place the ball. In all cases the
kicker's side must be behind the ball when it is kicked,
except the player who may be placing the ball for a place-
kick. In case of any infringement of this law, the Referee
shall order a scrummage at the mark. The opposite side
may come up to, and charge from anywhere on or behind
a line drawn through the mark and parallel to the goal-
lines, and may charge as soon as the catcher commences to
run or offers to kick or places the ball on the ground for a
place-kick, but in case of a drop-kick or punt, the kicker
may always draw back, and unless he has dropped the ball,

X

the opposite side must retire to the line of the mark. But
if any of the opposite side do charge before the player
having the ball commences to run or offers to kick, or the
ball has touched the ground for a place-kick (and this applies
to tries at goal as well as free kicks), provided the kicker
has not taken his kick, the charge may be disallowed.

IV.—PENALTIES.

Penalty Kicks for intentionally handling Ball or falling in Scrummage.

11.—Free kicks by way of penalties shall be awarded on
claims by the opposite side, if any player—

> (*a*) Intentionally either handles the ball, or falls down
> in a scrummage, or picks the ball out of a
> scrummage.

Not putting Ball down when held.

> (*b*) Having the ball, does not immediately put it down
> in front of him on it being held.

Not getting up or allowing to get up.

> (*c*) Being on the ground, does not immediately get up.
> (*d*) Prevents an opponent getting up.

Illegally Obstructing, etc.

> (*e*) Illegally tackles, charges, or obstructs, as in Law 8.

Unfairly putting Ball down.

(*f*) Wilfully puts the ball unfairly into a scrummage, or,
the ball having come out, wilfully shoves it forward with his
hands again into the scrummage.

Illegal Charge.

(*g*) Not himself running at the ball, charges or obstructs an opponent not holding the ball.

(*h*) Not in a scrummage wilfully obstructs his opponents' backs by standing on his opponents' side of the ball when it is in a scrummage.

(*i*) Being in a scrummage, lifts a foot from the ground before the ball has been put into such scrummage.

(*j*) Wilfully prevents the ball being fairly put into a scrummage.

The places of infringement shall be taken as the mark, and any one of the side granted the free kick may place or kick the ball.

V.—GENERAL.

Ball in Touch.

12.—The ball is in touch when it, or a player carrying it, touch or cross the touch-line; it shall then belong to the side opposite to that last touching it in the field of play, except when carried in. One of the side to whom the ball belongs shall bring it into play at the spot where it went into touch, by one of the following methods :—

(*a*) Bounding it on the field of play at right angles to the touch-line. After bounding it he may catch it, and then run with it, kick it, or pass it. When catching it he must have both feet in the field of play.

Throw-out.

(*b*) Throwing it out so as to alight at right angles to the touch-line, or

(*c*) Scrummaging it at any spot at right angles to the touch-line, between 5 and 15 yards from the place where it went into touch.

If the ball be not thrown out of touch, so as to alight at

right angles to the touch-line, the opposite side may bring it
out as in (*c*).

Try at Goal.

13.—When the side has scored a try, the ball shall be
brought from the spot where the try was gained into the
field of play in a line parallel to the touch-lines, such
distance as the placer thinks proper, and there he shall
place the ball for one of his side to try and kick a goal ;
this place-kick is governed by Law 10 as to charging, etc.,
the mark being taken as on the goal-line. It is the duty
of the defending side to see that the ball is taken out
straight.

Unfair Play, Allowing or Disallowing a Try.

The Referee shall award a try, if, in his opinion, one
would undoubtedly have been obtained but for unfair play
or interference of the defending side. Or, he shall dis-
allow a try, and adjudge a touch-down, if, in his opinion,
a try would undoubtedly not have been gained but for unfair
play or interference of the attacking side. In case of a try
so allowed, the kick at goal shall be taken at any point on
a line parallel to the touch-lines, and passing through the
spot where the ball was when such unfair play or interference took place.

Ball held in In-goal.

14.—If the ball, when over the goal-line and in possession
of a player, be fairly held by an opposing player before it is
grounded, it shall be scrummaged 5 yards from the goal-
line, opposite the spot where the ball was held.

Drop-out.

15.—After an unsuccessful try or touch-down, or if the
ball after crossing the goal-line go into touch-in-goal or

touch, or cross the dead-ball line, it shall be brought into play by means of a drop-out, when all the kicker's side must be behind the ball when kicked ; in case any are in front, the Referee shall order a scrummage on the 25 yards line, and equi-distant from the touch-lines.

Knock-on, Throw-forward.

16.—In case of a throw-forward or knock-on, the ball shall be at once brought back to where such infringement took place, and there put down, unless a fair catch has been made and claimed, or unless the opposite side gain an advantage. If the ball or a player running with the ball touches the Referee, it shall there be put down.

Pass or Carry Back over own Goal-line.

17.—If a player shall wilfully kick, pass, knock, or carry the ball back across his goal-line, and it there be made dead, the opposite side may claim that the ball shall be brought back, and a scrummage formed at the spot whence it was kicked, passed, knocked, or carried back. Under any other circumstances a player may touch the ball down in his own in-goal.

Hacking, Tripping.

18.—No HACKING, or HACKING OVER, or tripping up, shall be allowed under any circumstances. No one wearing projecting nails, iron plates, or gutta-percha on any part of his boots or shoes shall be allowed to play in a match.

Irregularities in In-Goal not otherwise provided for.

19.—In case of any law being infringed in in-goal by the attacking side, a touch-down shall be awarded, but where such breach is committed by the defending side, a scrummage shall be awarded 5 yards from the goal-line, opposite to the spot where the breach occurred.

Other Irregularities not provided for.

But in the case of any law being broken, or any irregularity of play occurring on the part of either side not otherwise provided for, the ball shall be taken back to the place where the breach of the law or irregularity of play occurred, and a scrummage formed there.

Close Time.

20.—There shall be an annual close time, during which it is illegal to play football where gate-money is taken, such close time being between April 20 and September 1.

REGULATIONS AUTHORIZED BY THE RUGBY UNION ON COUNTY QUALIFICATIONS.

1.—A man may play—

    (*a*) For the county in which he was born, or

    (*b*) For the county in which he has resided for the six months previous to the time of playing, or

    (*c*) For the county in which he is residing at school or college, either as pupil or master, at the time of playing, provided his residence at the school or college be in the same county.

    (*d*) For the county for which he played in season 1887-1888.

2.—A man shall still be qualified to play for a county, having previously qualified for and played for that county for three seasons, and not having subsequently played for any other county.

3.—No man shall play for more than one county during the same season.

4.—A man who is duly qualified and plays for a county in a certain season, may continue to play for that county during the remainder of that season, even though he loses his other qualifications.

5.—Should any question arise as to qualifications, the same shall be left to the decision of the Rugby Union Committee.

RULES AS TO PROFESSIONALISM.

Adopted at Rugby Union Meeting, September, 1895, which shall take the place of the Rules as to Professionalism, the " Insurance Laws," and the " Transfer Laws," which were in operation previously.

1.—Professionalism is illegal.

2.—Acts of professionalism are :

(1) By an individual—

A.—Asking, receiving, or relying on a promise, direct or implied, to receive any money consideration whatever, actual or prospective ; any employment or advancement ; any establishment in business ; or any compensation whatever for—

    (*a*) Playing football, or rendering any service to a football organization.

    (*b*) Training, or loss of time connected therewith.

    (*c*) Time lost in playing football or in travelling in connection with football.

    (*d*) Expenses in excess of the amount actually disbursed on account of reasonable hotel or travelling expenses.

B.—Transferring his services from one club to another in opposition to Rule 6.

C.—Playing for a club while receiving, or after having received from such club, any consideration whatever for acting as secretary, treasurer, or in any other

office, or for doing or for having done any work or
labour about the club's ground or in connection
with the club's affairs.

D.—Remaining on tour at his club's expense longer than
is reasonable.

E.—Giving or receiving any money testimonial. Or giving
or receiving any other testimonial, except under the
authority of this Union.

F.—Receiving any medal or other prize for any competition except under the authority of this Union.

G.—Playing on any ground where gate-money is taken :

    (*a*) During the close season.

    (*b*) In any match or contest where it is previously
    agreed that less than fifteen players on
    each side shall take part.

H.—Knowingly playing with or against any expelled or
suspended player or club.

I.—Refusing to give evidence or otherwise assist in carrying out these rules when requested by this Union to
do so.

J.—Being registered as, or declared a professional, or
suspended by any National Rugby Union, or by the
Football Association.

K.—Playing within eight days of any accident for which
he has claimed or received insurance compensation,
if insured under these rules.

L.—Playing in any benefit match connected directly or
indirectly with football.

M.—Knowingly playing or acting as referee or touch-
judge on the ground of an expelled or suspended
club.

(2) By a club or other organization :

A.—Paying or promising payment, or giving, offering,
or promising any inducement as to employment,

advancement, or establishment in business, or any compensation whatever to any player for—

    (*a*) Playing for that club.

    (*b*) Training, or for travelling expenses to or from any training resort, or for loss of time in connection with training.

    (*c*) Loss of time while playing or travelling in connection with football.

    (*d*) Hotel or travelling expenses in excess of the sum actually and reasonably disbursed.

B.—Receiving as a member a member of another club in opposition to Rule 6.

C.—Receiving or continuing as a member any one it may pay or have paid for either regular or occasional services.

D.—Paying for any of its teams, players, officials, or members on tour longer than a reasonable time ; or paying for more than a reasonable number.

E.—Giving from its funds, subscribing, or playing a match for any testimonial.

F.—Giving any medal or other prize for any competition except under the authority of this Union.

G.—Taking gate-money at any ground—

    (*a*) During the close season.

    (*b*) At any match or contest where it is previously agreed that less than fifteen players on each side shall take part.

H.—Knowingly playing or allowing its members to play with or against any expelled or suspended player or club.

I.—Refusing to produce its books or documents, or to allow its officials or members to give evidence, or to assist in carrying out these rules when requested by the Union to do so.

J.—Knowingly playing or admitting as a member, without the consent of the Union, any member or an expelled or suspended club, or any expelled or suspended player, or any person registered as or declared a professional or suspended by any National Rugby Union or by the Football Association.

K.—Knowingly allowing a player to play in its matches within eight days of any accident for which he has received or claimed insurance compensation, if insured under these rules.

L.—Playing or allowing its ground to be used for any benefit match connected directly or indirectly with football.

M.—Knowingly allowing its members or teams to play on the ground of any expelled or suspended club.

N.—Refusing to pay, within one month, any costs or expenses ordered by this Union for inquiries held under these rules.

3.—For offences under 2 (1), A, H, I, L, and M, an individual shall be expelled from all English clubs playing Rugby football, and shall not be eligible for re-election or election to any club. For offences under 2 (1), B, C, D, E, F, G, J, and K, an individual shall be suspended during the pleasure of this Union.

4.—For offences under 2 (2), A, D, H, I, L, M, and N, a club shall be expelled from this Union. For offences under 2 (2), B, C, E, F, G, J, and K, a club shall be suspended during the pleasure of this Union. Any club disregarding a sentence of suspension shall be liable to expulsion.

5.—When this Union is fully satisfied that any offence under 2 (2), A, D, H, I, L, M, and N, was of an accidental, trivial, or technical character, they may suspend instead of expel.

6.—When a player wishes to join a new club he may do so ; if this Union request it, he shall produce a letter from his old club stating that they have no objection ; on receipt of such letter this Union shall give the necessary permission, unless they believe there may have been collusion, or that illegal means have been employed to induce the player to join the new club, in which case they shall hold an inquiry. In case any club or clubs refuse to give such written permission, this Union must hold an inquiry, at the request of the player or of the club he wishes to join. If from any cause an inquiry be held, this Union shall have full power to order the payment of the costs of such inquiry, and of the clubs and witnesses, as it may think fit.

This Union may grant power to recognized governing bodies to increase the stringency of this rule, provided such proposed alterations be submitted to and approved of by it.

7.—A county or club may insure its players either through—

A.—A recognized insurance company, or

B.—A fund entirely set apart for insurance ; the accounts of such fund to be yearly audited by a professional auditor. Such audit to be made at the close of each season, and to be concluded, and the auditor's certificate lodged with this Union, not later than May 20 in each year, provided that :

> (*a*) Any injured player does not receive more than 6*s.* per week-day while injured.
>
> (*b*) Payments are only made on the certificate of a registered medical practitioner.
>
> (*c*) Any player does not play football within eight days of his accident. If he does so, no insurance compensation shall be paid.
>
> (*d*) Proper books of accounts be kept.

8.—This Union may hold inquiries into any alleged

breaches of these rules at its pleasure, and shall do so when requested by any club or member of a club, provided any such club or member make a preliminary deposit of £10, or such smaller sum as this Union may determine, to be accompanied by a preliminary written statement of the chief known facts. After any such inquiry, this Union may return the preliminary deposit, wholly or in part, and may order the expenses of such inquiry, of clubs and members implicated, and of witnesses, to be paid as it may determine.

9.—At all inquiries under Rules 6 and 8 correct notes must be taken.

10.—Any club, member, or player affected by any decision given by a county, union of counties, or university, under delegation of powers contained in Rule 11, may appeal direct to this Union. Such appeal must be made within ten days, and must be accompanied by a deposit of £50 and a written statement of the grounds of appeal. After any such appeal, this Union may return such deposit, wholly or in part, and may order the expenses of such inquiry, of club and members implicated, and of witnesses, to be paid as it may determine.

11.—This Union may delegate to recognized governing bodies, such as counties, union of counties, and universities, powers to act for it in such cases and under such regulations as it may determine. All powers so delegated, and the bodies to whom such delegation be made, shall be published annually in the official guide of this Union.

12.—This Union may appoint a sub-committee or committees to act on its behalf in all cases arising under these rules, giving such powers as it may determine.

13.—This Union shall have power to deal with all acts which it may consider as acts of professionalism, and which are not specifically provided for.

14.—Where the word " Union " is used in these rules, the

committee of this Union for the time being shall be understood, and, in the delegation of powers, the committee of the recognized governing body shall be understood. In case any difference of opinion arises as to the meaning of any of these rules, such meaning shall be decided by the committee of this Union, or, if it occurs at a general meeting, by the chairman thereof. Any such decision shall be entered in the minutes, and shall be accepted as the true meaning until otherwise interpreted by a two-thirds majority at a general meeting of this Union after due notice has been given.

DELEGATION OF POWERS.

The Rugby Union Committee have delegated to the following recognized governing bodies, namely, to the counties of Northumberland, Durham, Cumberland, Westmorland, Yorkshire, Lancashire, Cheshire, Middlesex, Kent, Surrey, Sussex, Hampshire, Gloucestershire, Somersetshire, Devonshire, and Cornwall ; to the Universities of Oxford and Cambridge ; to the Midland Counties' and Eastern Counties' Unions ; and to the Northern Federation (consisting of the counties of Northumberland, Durham, Cumberland and Westmorland, for any cases not exclusively in one of these counties, but within two or more of the four).

The following powers to act for them, namely :

A.—*Under Rule* 11 *in the Rules as to Professionalism.*

Under Rules 2, 3, and 4 all powers except—

(1) The power of reinstatement after suspension.

(2) The passing of sentence of expulsion.

If individuals or clubs are found guilty under 2 (1) A, H, J, L, or M, or 2 (2) A, H, J, L, M, or N, they must be at once temporarily suspended, and reported to the Rugby Union.

Under Rules 6, 7, and 8 all powers.

The Rugby Union Committee solely have the power of expelling. The Rugby Union Committee also solely have the power to reinstate after suspension.

B.—*Under the Laws of the Game*, the following powers :
Law 3 (*b*).

The above powers are only delegated to recognized governing bodies, when all individuals and clubs involved are under the jurisdiction of one governing body.

While delegating the above powers, the Rugby Union Committee wish it to be distinctly understood that the above recognized governing bodies have not the power or right to further delegate any of these powers.

The Rugby Union Committee have ruled that where the words "expelled or suspended club or player," or words to this effect, are used in the Rules as to Professionalism, they shall be read to include any professional club or player.

The Committee wish to specially draw the attention of county and club committees to the fact that recognized governing bodies have no power to sanction the formation of Leagues, or combination of clubs, and also to the alterations in bye-law 17, as to Leagues having to submit any alteration in or addition to their Laws or Rules, to this Union, and as to the power of this Union to forbid the continuance of any League.

The Committee have delegated to the New Zealand Union the power to carry out their regulations, and have given them the right to delegate such powers to other Bodies in New Zealand.

REGULATIONS FOR DECIDING THE COUNTY CHAMPIONSHIP.

Adopted at Annual General Meeting, September, 1895, and altered at Annual General Meeting, September, 1896.

Division of groups.

1.—NORTHERN, comprising Cheshire, Cumberland, Durham, Lancashire, Northumberland, Westmorland, and Yorkshire.

SOUTHERN, divided into

SOUTH WESTERN, comprising Cornwall, Devonshire, Gloucestershire, and Somersetshire.

SOUTH EASTERN—**A**, comprising Kent, Middlesex, Midland Counties, and Surrey ; and **B**, comprising Eastern Counties, Hampshire, and Sussex.

It shall be left to the Rugby Union Committee to define the area from which players are to be chosen for the Eastern Counties.

2.—(I.) The Northern Group winner shall be ascertained by means of matches between each member of the group and the others.

(II.) The Southern Group winner shall be ascertained by means of—

(*a*) Matches between each member of the South Western Division and the others ;

(*b*) Matches between each member of the South Eastern **A** Division and the others ;

(*c*) Matches between each member of the South Eastern **B** Division and the others ; followed by

(*d*) A match between the counties at the head of (II.) (*b*) and (II.) (*c*) ; and followed by

(*e*) A match between the counties at the head of (II.) (*a*) and (II.) (*d*).

3.—The winner of the Championship shall be ascertained

by means of a match between the two counties at the head of the Northern and Southern Groups respectively.

4.—Each match shall be decided by points. A win shall score two points, and a drawn game one point to each side. If in any case, owing to two or more counties scoring an equal number of points, a winner is not ascertained, the Rugby Football Union Committee may declare the winner, or, in their discretion, order another match or matches to be played.

5.—The matches referred to in Regulation 2 (II.), (*a*), (*b*), (*c*), and (*d*) must be played by January 20 ; and the matches referred to in Regulation 2 (I.) and (II.) (*e*), must be played by February 20 ; the date of the match for the ¡Championship shall be fixed by the Rugby Football Union Committee should the two counties interested fail to agree.

6.—The match for the Championship shall be played in the North of England, if North *v.* South has been played in the South, and *vice versâ ;* the home county having choice of ground. The nett proceeds of the match shall be equally divided between the two counties engaged.

7.—Regulation 1 shall not be varied except by the vote of a General Meeting.

8.—Any question which shall arise and is not above provided for, may be decided by the Rugby Football Union Committee.

9.—That the Rugby Union Committee may delegate to a Sub-Committee of their Body the exercise of all or any of the powers conferred on them by the above regulations.

BYE-LAWS OF THE INTERNATIONAL RUGBY FOOTBALL BOARD.

1.—The Board shall be called "THE INTERNATIONAL RUGBY FOOTBALL BOARD."

2.—The Board shall consist of twelve representatives—six from the Rugby Union, and two from each of the other Unions. The chairman, who shall have a casting vote, shall be appointed at each meeting, in regular rotation from the different Unions in their order of seniority.

3.—The Board shall meet annually at Manchester, or at such place as is agreed upon by all the Unions, in the third week of October in each year.

4.—All international matches shall be played under the laws approved of by this Board.

5.—In case of disputes in international matches, a committee of the Board, consisting of two representatives appointed by each Union, shall have absolute and exclusive jurisdiction. The Board shall have no power to interfere with the game as played within the limits of the different Unions.

6.—Notice of any proposed alteration in the laws of the game, or in the bye-laws of the Board, shall be sent to the hon. sec. at least four weeks before the annual meeting in October, and the hon. sec. shall intimate these proposals to the Unions at least three weeks before the meeting.

7.—The hon. sec. shall at any time convene a special meeting of the Board on receipt of a requisition from the hon. secs. of at least two of the Unions. The purpose for which the meeting is desired shall be intimated to the different Unions at least three weeks before the said meeting.

8.—If the chairman entitled for the time being to preside shall on the occasion of any appeal happen to be a representative of either of the disputing Unions, his chairmanship

Y

shall be postponed in favour of, and take order next after, the chairmanship of the first neutral Union entitled by rotation to furnish a chairman.

9.—The Referee at any match shall be ineligible to act as a representative at the meeting called to settle any dispute arising out of that match.

10.—No alteration in the laws of the game or the bye-laws of the Board shall be made at any meeting called for that purpose, unless by a majority of at least three-fourths of the representatives present.

11.—All expenses incurred in connection with the Board shall be equally defrayed by the Unions ; but in the case of a committee appointed under Bye-law 5, all hotel and travelling expenses shall be equally defrayed by the disputing Unions.

12.—All decisions of the Board or committee shall be accepted as final.

NATIONAL QUALIFICATION.

There is no definition controlling any player's choice as to the country for which he shall play. The International Board in 1894 decided, at Leeds, that no player should in future play for more than one country, but did not proceed further.

PRINTED BY WILLIAM CLOWES AND SONS, LIMITED, LONDON AND BECCLES

Also available by Paul R. Spiring:

*On the Trail of Arthur Conan Doyle:
An Illustrated Devon Tour*

**by Brian W. Pugh &
Paul R. Spiring**

**ISBN-13: 978-1846241987 (English)
ISBN-13: 978-3981132755 (German)
ISBN-13: 978-1904312482 (Spanish)**

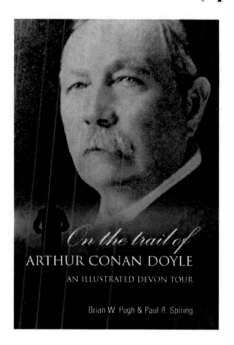

*"Its succinct account of Conan Doyle's association with
Devon and with George Turnavine Budd and Bertram
Fletcher Robinson is invaluable, and just to follow the
Devon Tour on paper is fascinating."*

The Sherlock Holmes Journal (Spring 2008).

Also available from MX Publishing Ltd:

Bertram Fletcher Robinson: A Footnote
to The Hound of the Baskervilles

by **Brian W. Pugh &**
Paul R. Spiring

ISBN-13: 978-1904312406 (Paperback)
ISBN-13: 978-1904312413 (Hardcover)

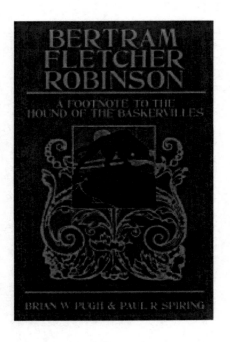

"A full scale biography of Fletcher Robinson. Being first
in their field allows the authors a virtual blank canvas for
their word painting, and this they use to no little effect."

The Sherlock Holmes Journal (Winter 2008).

Also available from MX Publishing Ltd:

*Aside Arthur Conan Doyle: Twenty Original
Tales by Bertram Fletcher Robinson*

Compiled by Paul R. Spiring

ISBN-13: 978-1904312529

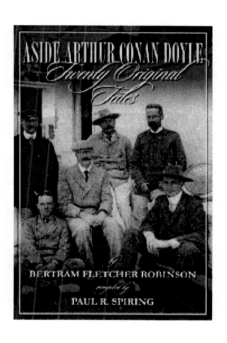

*"The collection proves that Fletcher Robinson was more
than capable of producing good work and would probably
have gone on to greater things had his life not been cut
short."*

**The Weekend Supplement of the
*Western Morning News*** (14 March 2009).

Also available from MX Publishing Ltd:

The World of Vanity Fair
by Bertram Fletcher Robinson

Compiled by Paul R. Spiring

ISBN-13: 978-1904312536

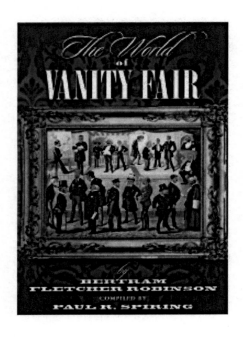

"Every now and then, you comes across a really
sumptuous book, where just turning and looking at the
pages takes you into another world. Such is the case with
this one."

The Bookbag (May 2009).

Also available from MX Publishing Ltd:

**Bobbles & Plum: Four Satirical Playlets
by Bertram Fletcher Robinson and
PG Wodehouse**

Compiled by Paul R. Spiring

ISBN-13: 978-1904312581

*"The discovery of four satirical 'playlets' by PG
Wodehouse, seen by the public for the first time in 100
years this weekend, prove that the humorist – who is often
viewed as apolitical – had a strong interest in public
affairs from his youth."*

The Observer (26 July 2009).

Also available from MX Publishing Ltd:

For College, Club & Country – A History of Clifton Rugby Football Club

**by Patrick Casey &
Dr. Richard Hale**

ISBN-13: 978-1904312758

"Richly illustrated with team photographs over more than 100 years, this is a fascinating piece of social history based around one of the oldest rugby clubs in the country."

The Bookbag (November 2009).

Also available from MX Publishing Ltd:

Arthur Conan Doyle, Sherlock Holmes and Devon:
A Complete Tour Guide & Companion

by Brian W. Pugh, Paul R. Spiring
and Dr. Sadru Bhanji

ISBN-13: 978-1904312864

For details about other available titles from MX
Publishing Ltd., please enquire at you local bookstore or
visit www.mxpublishing.co.uk. For more information
about Bertram Fletcher Robinson, please visit
www.bfronline.biz.

Lightning Source UK Ltd.
Milton Keynes UK
23 February 2010

150464UK00001B/3/P